Sugar Ray Leonard

Also by James Haskins and published by Robson Books:

THE COTTON CLUB

Sugar Ray Leonard

Jim Haskins

Robson Books

First published in Great Britain in 1989 by Robson Books Ltd, Bolsover House, 5-6 Clipstone Street, London W1P 7EB.

British Library Cataloguing in Publication Data

Haskins, James *1941–*
Sugar Ray Leonard
1. Boxing. Leonard, Sugar Ray, 1956–
I. Title
796.8'3'0924

ISBN 0 86051 501 X

Typeset by Concept, Crayford, England

Printed in Great Britain by Billing & Son Ltd., Worcester

To Joseph

Contents

Acknowledgements

I am grateful for the help of Colonel Hull of the AAU Boxing Commission, Nancy Opel of the Baltimore *Sun*, Patricia Allen-Brown, Laurel Burns, Ann L. Kalkhoff and Kathy Benson.

Introduction

THERE HAS NEVER been a fighter quite like Sugar Ray Leonard. In a time when the sport of boxing was dominated by heavyweights he, almost single-handed, elevated the lighter weight classes to popularity and large purses and virtually dominated the game in the late 1970s and early 1980s. In a game often called the blood sport, and frequently criticized as being no sport at all, Leonard has shown that in the right hands it becomes the sweet science, as *New Yorker* writer A. J. Liebling once wrote. Leonard has also shown that a boxer need not be 'owned' by promoters, managers and trainers to be successful, and that a boxer's career can be operated much like a corporation, independent of the image of crooked deals and cigar-smoke-filled rooms with which boxing has long been afflicted.

For his independence, and for his success, Sugar Ray Leonard has consistently been criticized and has never been fully accepted by the international boxing fraternity. Charges that he has always had it too easy and has never really paid his dues have dogged him throughout his career; and indeed, such charges have at times been well-founded. Hardly alone in retiring from the ring with some frequency, he has been singularly successful in returning to fight in matches of his own choosing rather than those that boxing tradition dictated.

Grudgingly, the boxing world admits that it needs a fighter like Sugar Ray Leonard, the personification of the pugilist in a world of pugs. But Leonard shares with less classy fighters a characteristic that more than any other reason explains why he has come out of retirement three times despite being a multi-millionaire and despite having suffered serious eye problems; like the most unsophisticated club fighter, he doesn't feel respected unless he is in the ring proving that he deserves respect. It was in the ring that a shy, skinny kid who was cruelly teased by older, more athletic brothers and ignored by a disappointed father proved them all wrong, and in his adult life he has constantly sought to relive that experience, finding reasons, real or imagined, to prove himself over, and over, and over again.

1

A Most Unlikely Fighter

UNTIL HE WAS fourteen years old, Sugar Ray Leonard did not seem to be the type of kid who would ever get interested in boxing. He was a shy loner, seemingly too insecure to put himself on the line. He was also skinny, and strenuous physical activity, except for somersaults, was the last thing that interested him. People now say that Sugar Ray Leonard is a born boxer, and indeed he has made that statement about himself, but no one, least of all Leonard himself, had any inkling of his native talent before he was a teenager.

Ray Charles Leonard was born 17 May, 1956, in Wilmington, North Carolina, where his father, Cicero Leonard, a former Navy cook, worked in the local Coca-Cola plant. Ray was the fifth child and fourth son born to Cicero and Getha Leonard, who liked the singing of the blind pianist Ray Charles and named her newest son in honour of the star. Some day, she told her friends and family, the little boy might become a singing star, too.

There were a lot of dreams in the Leonard household, but little reality on which to base them. Wilmington was a typical Southern town where blacks had to keep their place and where there were few opportunities for education or advancement. The elder Leonards were concerned about the poor schooling their children would inevitably receive and about their own seeming inability to get ahead. One day in 1960, Cicero Leonard walked home from work, packed up his family, and moved them all to Washington, DC.

At the time, the nation's capital was as racially segregated as any city in the Deep South, with statutes requiring blacks to sit at the back of public buses and streetcars, whites-only restaurants and water fountains, and other forms of *de jure* segregation. Ray had his first experience of racism in that city a few years later. He wandered into a small café not far from the Capitol one day, intending to ask for a drink of water. A man behind the counter shouted, 'No niggers in here! No goddamned niggers in here! Get out!' Frightened, Ray ran all the way home, and when his mother returned from work that evening he tearfully told her what had happened. She listened to him and then paused for a moment, trying to find the right words. Then she said quietly, 'Listen, little Ray, there's lots of bad folks in this world. Some of them are white, like that mean old fellow, but some of them are Negroes like you. You just try to avoid as many of them as you can, no matter what colour they are; but the best thing you can do is not be one of them.' Ray was deeply struck by the simple wisdom of his mother's words and henceforth regarded them as the best advice he had ever heard about how to get along in life.

In Washington, DC, the Leonards soon found out that housing was more expensive, and more downmarket than back in Wilmington. They had to cram into a small apartment on Avenue L. But there were far more employment opportunities, and both Cicero and Getha Leonard quickly found jobs, he working 2 a.m. to 10 a.m. at a produce market and she working nights as a nursing assistant in a convalescent home. With those schedules, one of them was around to watch the children except for a few hours in the early morning.

The Leonard children learned early not to expect a great deal of individual attention from their parents, particularly after the arrival of Ray's two younger sisters, Sharon and Sandy. Each child had his or her responsibilities from the time they could walk, and the more outgoing and aggressive ones fared the best. As the youngest boy, Ray never seemed to be able to match the physical prowess of his three older brothers, Roy, Kenny and Roger. Nor did he have their mischievous personalities, which frequently got them into trouble but which did garner them some much-needed attention. But he was a happy child, always smiling, and so quiet that sometimes his mother almost forgot he was there. She loved him for never having to worry about him.

After entering school, Ray realized for the first time how poor he and his family were. In their neighbourhood on Avenue L, everyone was as poor, if not poorer. But at school Ray encountered children who obviously had much more than he. Other kids had new clothes for the start of school, while Ray always wore hand-me-downs from Roger, who was three years older. Other kids could afford the dollar everyone was supposed to bring for class field trips, but there was never a dollar to spare in the Leonards' budget, so Ray would stay home. Sometimes there wasn't enough lunch money for all the Leonard children. But even as a youngster, Ray recognized how hard his parents were trying – between them, they sometimes held down four and five jobs at a time – and he never complained.

When they weren't in school or doing household chores, Ray's brothers were out playing sports, all kinds of sports, from basketball to baseball to track. Ray wasn't interested. He sat around the house reading comics. Once, when he was about seven, he accompanied Roger to the local Boys' Club, where there was a boxing programme, and watched Roger spar with another boy. Every time Roger was hit, Ray shut his eyes tight. An instructor tried to get Ray involved by strapping a pair of gloves on him and shoving him in the direction of another seven-year-old who was similarly equipped, and who was obviously more prepared for combat than Ray was. 'I thought the kid was going to kill me,' Ray recalled years later. He survived the brief contest, but suffered a splitting headache and decided that boxing was not for him.

Ray did have a nice singing voice, and with his mother's encouragement he joined the local church choir. That he could sing well gave him some sense of accomplishment, but his brothers looked at him as if being in the choir was not the sort of activity a normal boy would engage in.

By the time he was about nine, Ray had begun to feel that he should excel in something physical, if only to prevent his brothers from teasing him. So, with some neighbourhood boys he began to practise his version of gymnastics. There were a number of abandoned houses in the neighbourhood, and the boys would drag old mattresses out of the houses and line them up in back of a two-storey house. Then they would go up to the roof and jump from it down on to the mattresses. Ray got so he could do a flip in the air before he landed. Unfortunately, his brothers regarded this activity as kids' play and were not impressed.

When Ray was eleven, he lost even that modest physical outlet, for the family moved out of the city to Seat Pleasant, Maryland, and to a neighbourhood where there were no abandoned buildings and no old mattresses to use as trampolines. Hardly had the shy, introverted Ray begun to adjust to a new school and a new district when the family moved again, this time to their own house on Barlowe Road in Palmer Park, Maryland.

On Barlowe Road, money was as tight as ever in the Leonard household, because now there were mortgage payments to meet; but the security, not to mention the pride, of owning their own home affected the entire family. Cicero Leonard walked a little taller, and so did the rest. Ray, for one, felt it would be easier adjusting to yet another new school when he could walk into that new school knowing he was not going to be one of the poorest kids there.

Because he was such a loner, adjusting to new surroundings wasn't all that difficult for Ray. He simply remained in his shell. He recalled years later that the most he ever said to most people was 'Hi', and that he chose to be by himself because he had so little to say. Not for him the fighting for territory that marks the experiences of most new kids on the block or at school. When teased or challenged, Ray simply fled. He actually adjusted better and more quickly to his new neighbourhood in Palmer Park than he had to the two new places to which his family had moved earlier because of the overtures made by Derrik Holmes, a kid about his age. Derrik was outgoing and very popular, and immediately took Ray in tow, including him in his activities as a matter of course. Ray, eager to be around his new friend, was also eager to be included.

Following Derrik's lead, Ray began to play basketball and to go roller-skating after school and at weekends. Ray's older brother, Roger, was delighted that his young brother was coming out of his shell, and suggested that he should join the wrestling team. Ray was game, but a couple of contests persuaded him that he was not a wrestler. At the risk of alienating both friend and brother, Ray declined to pursue wrestling.

Next, he tried cross-country running, but at an early meet he suffered a painful pulled thigh muscle and was forced to drop out. He was horribly embarrassed and shortly thereafter he quit the team, much to the consternation of his family and friends.

He didn't even pursue his gymnastics career very long after he arrived in Palmer Park. While the area was not flush with abandoned houses and mattresses, there was gymnastics equipment at the junior high school that Ray attended, and he happily performed his flips to the delight of his gym teachers. One day, however, a gym teacher chose Ray to demonstrate a particularly difficult manoeuvre in which Ray would run up to him, jump into his hands and flip over into a backward somersault. Ray had never done any sort of backward somersault before, but he didn't want to appear chicken. He tried the stunt. He was all right until the teacher flipped him over into the air. Then, suddenly, he became terrified, and having lost his concentration he failed to negotiate the flip. He landed with a thud on his head, felt a strange sensation run through his body, and began to cry, embarrassing himself to the point of mortification.

After that experience, Ray decided that he was simply not cut out for athletics of any kind. He recalled during an interview with Lawrence Linderman for *Playboy*, 'As I told my mother, I could have broken my neck, so there had to be something better for me to do. Of course, I didn't find it right away. I started hanging around the house after school, waiting for Mother to cook dinner. My brothers kept teasing me and really hurt my feelings.'

Cicero Leonard didn't tease his youngest son, but he was definitely worried. Ray was so shy, such a loner. Except for Derrik, he had no close friends, and even Roger, whom Ray continued to idolize, could not get him outside to play any kind of sport. It wasn't that he was a bad kid. On the contrary, he never caused his parents any trouble. Occasionally, one or another Leonard child would act up at school, but never Ray Charles Leonard. Cicero Leonard wished his son *would* act up once in a while – do something to show that he was a normal teenager. The older Leonard found it hard to relate to his youngest son. He worried about the kid's social adjustment. He was afraid Ray was a sissy. No doubt Ray sensed his father's disapproval, which didn't help the almost non-existent relationship the two had.

Around that same time, when Ray was fourteen, a recreation centre was built in Palmer Park to give youngsters in the mostly black, working-class area a healthy outlet for their energies. Too many of them loitered on the street corners, took drugs, and engaged in vandalism and petty thievery. The local shopping centre had become a hangout for bored and restless kids, and drug selling and prostitution flourished there at night. Merchants complained that the kids were scaring away customers and, citing statistics that petty crime had increased, lobbied for a recreation centre. The Parks Department opened the Palmer Park Recreation Center in 1970 to a great fanfare. The facility had a well-equipped gym, with a concentration on basketball, which was the sport of choice for most Palmer Park youths.

Roger Leonard was a notable exception. According to Ray, as soon as the family arrived in Palmer Park, Roger started walking around with a pair of boxing gloves slung over his shoulder. He went often to the local shopping centre, but not to hang out; he was always looking for some guys who would help him set up a makeshift ring and take him on. When the Palmer Park Recreation Center opened, Roger was delighted to learn that one of the volunteer coaches was a former boxer.

Dave Jacobs had been a fervent supporter of the Center and was now one of the first to volunteer as a coach. He had a deep interest in the young people of his community and a firm conviction that sport was the best way to channel their energies, as it had been for him. He credited sports with helping him to avoid the pitfalls of crime and boredom when he was a youngster, and he was especially fond of boxing. In 1949, as a young man, he had won a district Amateur Athletic Union featherweight title and had subsequently turned professional, doing well as a middleweight. When he married and started a family, however, he decided that he needed a more secure job and a steady income and had gone to work delivering merchandise for a pharmacy, shelving his dreams of money and glory in the ring. Over the years, he had naturally gravitated to local gyms and boxing clubs, giving to younger men the benefit of the wisdom and experience he could no longer use. While boosting the idea of a recreation centre, he had quietly harboured thoughts of starting a boxing team there, and when Roger Leonard showed up with his boxing gloves, Jacobs had reasons other than selfish ones to push for a boxing programme.

Ollie Dunlap, the Center's director, listened to Jacobs and was willing to start a boxing team, but when he approached the Parks Department for funding he was rebuffed. Boxing wasn't especially popular in Palmer Park, and in the nation, at that time.

The popularity of boxing in America over the years has existed in direct proportion to the supply of talented fighters as well as promoters willing to spend the money and take the risks involved in staging the big fights. There did not seem to be many fighters or promoters like that around in the early 1970s. Gone were the days of Schmeling and Louis, Rocky Graziano, Rocky Marciano, Jake LaMotta. Back in the 1920s and 1930s every city and town of any size had its small boxing clubs, which served as training grounds for young fighters. Over the years, the number of clubs had steadily declined. Big-city gyms and recreation programmes still included boxing, as did many high schools and colleges, but there was much more activity on the amateur level than in professional boxing.

Consequently, there were fewer opportunities for the general public to watch boxing matches. Back in the 1950s when television was new and boxing was still popular, matches were frequently televised, further boosting the popularity of the game. But as greater variety in television programming developed, less air-time was available for fight broadcasts. The racial make-up of boxing also played a role in its popularity, or lack thereof. It had long been an integrated sport, a claim which the more popular team sports could not make until the 1940s when the colour line was broken in baseball. Indeed, by the 1950s, boxing had become dominated by blacks, and given the racial make-up of the majority of the public, that spelt bad news for the sport's continued popularity, especially on television. A fight between a white and a black might not bring out the best humanitarian feelings in the audience, but at least it generated excitement. Witness the Jack Johnson – Jim Jeffries bout in 1910, or the two contests between Joe Louis and Max Schmeling. But a contest between two blacks did not interest most whites, many of whom felt that boxing had been taken over by blacks. They turned their attention to sports like football, which were still lily-white.

Boxing had only itself to blame for some of its lack of popularity. It was a brutal sport, closely identified with organized crime. The scandals in boxing since the Second World War were legion – fixed fights, crooked fight promotion schemes – and frequently deserved. The fact that there was no single international boxing organization to formulate one standard set of rules only enhanced the sport's reputation for sleaziness.

Until 1920, many countries, and nearly every US state, had their own boxing organizations and rules. Since it was primarily an amateur sport, this lack of organization did not present serious problems. The trouble started when boxing became a professional sport. In 1920 New York State took steps to professionalize boxing, which had been legal since 1896, by creating the New York State Athletic Commission. That same year, a rival organization, the private National Boxing Association, claiming membership of thirteen states, arose and immediately challenged the state-run group. The two competing organizations sometimes recognized different boxers as world champions in the same weight class, causing the sport, and its champions, to be regarded with considerable scepticism by the population as a whole.

This confusion was not unique to the USA. Similar problems arose in other parts of the world. Arguments over voting power kept the issue in the air until the early 1960s when a movement was made to unify world professional boxing with the creation, in 1963, of the World Boxing Council (WBC). The WBC comprised the British, Continental European, North American, South American, Oriental, Pan Pacific and African Boxing Federations. Almost at the same time, the National Boxing Association, ever the rival, changed its name to the World Boxing Association (WBA), which took some nerve, since its jurisdiction only covered some parts of the United States. In the US, some states joined the WBC, some joined the WBA, and some joined both to be safe.

The two rival organizations continue today to vie jealously with one another and with the 1983 International Boxing Federation for power, prestige and purses. They do, however, follow the same general rules as to weight class. Eight major weight divisions are universally recognized:

Flyweight (not over 112 lb)
Bantamweight (not over 118 lb)
Featherweight (126 lb)
Lightweight (135 lb)
Welterweight (147 lb)
Middleweight (160 lb)
Light Heavyweight (175 lb)
Heavyweight (over 175 lb)

In addition, three 'junior' weight divisions are generally recognized for boxers whose weight falls between two of the various divisions – Junior Lightweight (130 lb), Junior

Welterweight (140 lb), and Junior Middleweight (154 lb). Yet another weight category was adopted in 1988, the Super Middleweight (168 lb).

Rules for ring size, length of rounds, and what constitutes a knockout or a technical knockout are the same in the WBA, WBC and IBF, although in the WBA title fights are twelve rounds instead of fifteen rounds in length. But they continue to guard their independence jealously, and the existence of two 'world' and one 'international' boxing associations continues to hamper professional boxing today, just as the two rival organizations did back in the early 1970s when the lack of a unified organization in the pro game added to the other myriad problems from which boxing suffered.

Not since 1964 had any fighter sparked the interest and imagination of the public and caused promoters to risk all that was necessary to stage a big fight. In that year, a young heavyweight named Cassius Clay took the crown from Charles 'Sonny' Liston with a showbiz style not seen in the fight game for a long time. Not only was Clay an exceptionally talented fighter who moved much more quickly than the average heavyweight, he was a natural 'media personality': Handsome – 'Pretty', as he called himself – and cocky and eminently quotable. Sports writers loved to quote such unabashed pronouncements as 'I'm the greatest,' and his funny poems – 'Float like a butterfly, sting like a bee . . .' Clay could have brought boxing back to popularity single-handed, and in fact he did. But he became more notorious than famous after he converted to the version of Islam preached by a small black sect out of Chicago called The Nation of Islam, changed his name to Muhammad Ali, and in 1967 refused induction into the US Army citing his religious beliefs. In response, and in one of the rare occasions when they agreed, both the WBA and WBC stripped him of his heavyweight title.

In 1970, Ali announced that he was making a comeback, and in 1971 he challenged world heavyweight champion, Joe Frazier. The bout garnered more excitement than the boxing world had seen since Ali's fall from grace, but after he lost to Frazier by decision most observers pronounced him a has-been. No other fighter had Ali's charisma, and the fight game remained in the doldrums.

Without inspiring stars, most people didn't think much of boxing, and the decision-makers at the Palmer Park Parks Department could not see the point of funding an unpopular sport. When Dave Jacobs and Ollie Dunlap persisted, they managed to secure a small amount of seed money for a boxing programme – enough to cover the price of a couple of punching bags. Dave Jacobs determined to raise the rest of the money that was needed, and so he got small donations from local merchants to buy boxing gloves and scavenged junkyards for a dresser mirror in front of which the kids could practise their shadow boxing. He took strips of tape and marked out a 'ring' on the Center's basketball court. He then furnished that makeshift ring with tumbling mats. Such amenities as a raised canvas floor would have to come later. In the meantime, Jacobs simply decided that the first skill he would teach his young fighters was *balance*.

Ray's older brother, Roger, was one of the first local kids to join the boxing programme. Derrik Holmes was not far behind. Ray demurred for a time, but after a while he decided he could no longer put up with his brothers' constant, teasing question, 'Where are your trophies, kid?' He joined the boxing programme at the Palmer Park Recreation Center. Dave Jacobs later recalled his first impression of Ray Leonard – a shy, uncoordinated, skinny kid who didn't seem to have a shred of self-confidence, who wouldn't even look him straight in the eye. When asked to put on a pair of gloves and strike a boxing pose, Ray put his fists up in the air, copying the poses he had seen of boxers who were famous fifty years before. Jacobs stifled a laugh. The kid was going to need a lot of work.

The first thing Ray discovered was that boxing was a painful contact sport. He got headaches, nosebleeds and black eyes. He would come home from the Center, eat dinner, and immediately go to bed, taunted unmercifully by his brothers. But he kept at it. He was determined, as he told Lawrence Linderman, 'to show my brothers that I was a boy like them, that I was rough, too'.

For several months Ray went through sheer torture, grimly determined to show that he was tough. While Dave Jacobs wanted him to build up his strength and spar infrequently with fighters of comparable ability, Ray seemed to invite punishment. He actually challenged David Jerry, an older, hard-hitting boxer who had already knocked Roger Leonard around. Jerry weighed about 180. Ray tipped the scales at around 128. It was a short bout. Ray was knocked down and suffered a bloody nose. Frustrated as well as hurt, he cried.

But something made him stay with it. To this day, he is hard put to it to explain the source of that bull-headed determination to keep getting back into the ring after every knockdown. His best explanation is that he was so profoundly hurt by his brothers' teasing, and perhaps also by his father's despairing attitude towards him, that he could not quit.

Little by little, he was improving. Dave Jacobs could see that. In just a few weeks, Ray's coordination had improved, and he had begun to develop a dancing style like Muhammad Ali's, because he still didn't like being hit. Jacobs noted that he was a quick study and rarely had to be shown a technique more than once. More surprising, Ray seemed to become a different person in the ring. He looked his opponent straight in the eye and moved with a confidence that he did not show outside the ring. Jacobs was beginning to pay attention to the skinny, shy kid who still would not look him in the eye.

For his part, although he was in almost constant pain, Ray could feel himself getting more skilled and stronger. At last he had found something he believed he could do, and that knowledge made an immediate difference in his life. He no longer moped around home after school. He went straight to the Recreation Center. He got up at 5 o'clock in the morning to run around the ballfield behind his house with Derrik Holmes and other youngsters in the boxing programme.

Although Getha Leonard was pleased to see her

youngest son involved in something outside himself, she could not get used to the idea of his boxing. It seemed like the last thing on earth that would interest the small, baby-faced Ray, who came home at least once or twice a week with a black eye or a bruised lip. She could hardly refrain from bursting into tears when she saw him like that. Her other sons had always been rugged and athletic, and for them bruises were a matter of course. But Ray was different and always had been. Mrs Leonard kept her own counsel, however, sensing that this was something her youngest son needed to do in order to prove himself.

The hardest thing for her to accept was Ray's quitting the church choir when he was fourteen and a half. He had done well in the choir, as had two of his sisters; people said he sounded like the rock 'n' roll singer, Sam Cooke. Ray couldn't bring himself to tell his mother that he simply could not control his voice any more and that it was embarrassing to let out a squeak when it was least expected. 'Mom,' he explained, 'I put the singing into swinging.' But this was small comfort to Getha Leonard.

No one in the family took Ray's boxing seriously. He begged his brothers to come to the Center to watch him, but they just laughed at him. They had made up their minds about their little brother. Besides, they had other things to do. Cicero Leonard was equally uninterested. He, too, had formed an opinion about his youngest son that nothing, seemingly, could change. Oh, he gave the kid credit for trying, but Ray just wasn't the type of son he could understand. Never had been. He wasn't cut from the same cloth as the rest of the men in the Leonard line.

Cicero Leonard's father had been a sharecropper, and a man of legendary strength. It was said that he could make a stubborn mule go down on its knees with just one punch. Cicero Leonard inherited his father's strength, and when he was a boy he dreamed of growing up to be like his boxing idol, Joe Louis, who was a symbol of hope for downtrodden black Americans in the 1930s. While serving in the Navy, Leonard had fought as a middleweight in military competitions, losing only one out of 70 fights, and had circumstances been more favourable he might have had a shot at a pro career. But like Dave Jacobs, he had married and started a family and soon put aside his dreams in order to live up to his responsibilities as a provider. When his older sons showed an interest in, and aptitude for, sports, and especially when Roger took up boxing, Cicero Leonard had allowed himself to dream again. But he had little patience for the pretensions to boxing of his youngest son.

Cicero Leonard was aware that he did not know Ray very well. They had never been close, and for years there had been an invisible wall between them. Ray was so different, so hard to understand. But the older man did feel he knew what it took to be a boxer, and he was convinced that Ray did not have it. Cicero Leonard said he was too busy to go down to the Recreation Center and watch Ray box. In actuality, he believed he was shielding himself and his son from the disappointment he was sure he would feel.

In the absence of any support from his father, Ray turned more and more to Dave Jacobs, who taught him not only about boxing but also about life. A firm believer in training the bodies as well as the minds of young athletes, Jacobs taught mental and moral discipline, constantly preached clean living, faith in God, and the Golden Rule. Coming from him, this preaching was a lot easier for the kids to take than it would have been from their own parents, and Jacobs had considerable influence on the lives of many of the youngsters who frequented the Palmer Park Recreation Center.

They liked and respected him because he so obviously had their interests in mind. His was still a volunteer position at the Center, and yet he put in hours not just training the youngsters but raising money to support the boxing programme, which was still a low priority in the eyes of the Parks Department officials who controlled funding. In a matter of a few months, Jacobs had boys ready to compete in local amateur contests, and to raise money for transportation and fees he and his wife held benefit suppers, for which Mrs Jacobs cooked cases of chicken and spare ribs and made pounds of greens and potato salad. Ollie Dunlap, director of the Center, pitched in as well, soliciting donations from local merchants. As time went on, the performance of the kids justified such donations.

When they had started the boxing programme, Dunlap and Jacobs had not expected to turn out great fighters; they had simply wanted to give local youngsters a reason to come in off the streets. But the boys did so well in local amateur contests that both men began to realize that they had underestimated the boxing talent in Palmer Park. They stepped up their efforts to get the kids involved in amateur competitions, knowing that this would not only benefit the kids but also the boxing programme at the Center.

Ray was boxing in these local competitions by the time he was fifteen. He had put on about 25 pounds since entering the programme, and most of it was pure muscle, for he was still skinny. He never shirked his roadwork and was always on time for sparring sessions. He kept up with his schoolwork because one of the rules was that a kid had to maintain a C average. The Center still did not have a real boxing ring, but this proved no drawback for Ray or for the other boys. If anything, it prepared them better than boys for whom balance was not so crucial. Ray began boxing in local competitions, and winning his bouts, which gave him confidence. His sweetest victory was over David Jerry, who had given him a bloody nose just a few months before. Perhpas it was this new-found confidence that communicated itself to Cicero Leonard the time he finally agreed to watch his youngest son fight.

Cicero Leonard went reluctantly. He was still half convinced that his son would lose and embarrass both of them. But what he saw that Saturday night amazed him and erased all scepticism from his mind. Ray in the ring was aggressive and confident. In fact, Ray in the ring was an entirely different personality. His eyes were steely, his jaw set – it was an expression his father had never seen on his face before. And his boxing! The kid was a natural – quick, smart, able to take advantage of his opponent's mistakes. Ray won that fight, and his father felt a pride he had never thought his youngest son would evoke in him. The kid really had something! Why hadn't he ever seen it? Of course, he knew the answer to that question – he'd never paid enough attention to Ray to know. The relationship between father and son improved markedly after that night, and henceforth Cicero Leonard took a keen interest in Ray's career. Ray's older brothers changed their attitude toward him as well. It had taken more than a year, but at last young Ray Leonard had proved himself to the people who were most important to him.

In the spring of 1971, fifteen-year-old Ray Leonard went up against Bobby Magruder, out of the Hillcrest Heights Boys' Club a few miles away from Palmer Park. Magruder was nineteen or twenty at the time and reputed to be one of the most talented fighters in the area, having already seen successful competition in the Junior Olympics and the Golden Gloves tournaments. There was considerable local rivalry between the two recreation Centers, and between the two towns, so when the match was made it caused great excitement.

Ray was nervous about the match, and when at the last minute Dave Jacobs had to leave to do a family errand, Ray was suddenly frightened. Fortunately, Janks Morton, Jacobs' assistant in the Palmer Park Recreation Center boxing programme, stepped in. 'You're gonna beat him Ray. Just keep cool and move,' Morton advised, and Ray followed that advice, winning a three-round decision and considerable local fame. 'From then on,' Ray Leonard recalled later, 'I knew I was a fighter'.

Remarkably, in a little over a year, Ray Leonard had changed from a skinny, uncoordinated kid to a young boxer to be reckoned with. The problem for Jacobs and Morton now was to find competitors who would challenge him. Finding few real challengers locally, Jacobs and Morton began to think in national terms.

Even the local competitions were conducted under the auspices of the Amateur Athletic Union of the United States (AAU). This nation-wide, non-profit organization set standards for amateur competitions in most sports and sponsored events at the national level. By the latter part of

1971, Ray was being groomed for national competition.

In 1972 he competed in and won the annual Golden Gloves championship in the lightweight class. Later in the year he reached the quarter-finals in the AAU National Tournament, beating fighters five and ten years older than himself. In fact, Ray was so good that he was allowed to join the 1972 AAU national team that competed against teams from other countries.

At the age of sixteen, Ray was not supposed to be on that team. By international amateur athletic rules, the minimum age for competition was seventeen. But AAU Boxing Chairman Rollie Schwartz decided not to make an issue of Ray's age. Schwartz went through the formalities, asking Ray how old he was, and when Ray put on an innocent face and said seventeen, Schwartz did not question him further, for in his opinion the national team needed Ray, no matter what his age was. Schwartz believed that Ray Leonard was the best amateur lightweight boxer in the United States, and with competitors like the Russian national team, the US team needed its best fighters. Besides, the men who were on that AAU national team would get a chance to be in the 1972 Olympics.

Ray Leonard had his first experience of international competition when the Russian amateur boxing team came to Las Vegas, Nevada. He also had his first taste of domestic travel, which he loved. Seeing the names of stars on the marquees of the big clubs on the Las Vegas Strip, and actually seeing comedian Redd Foxx and former welterweight champion Sugar Ray Robinson at ringside was a thrill for him. He also discovered, however, that he missed the familiar things of home – his mother's cooking, his own bed, the daily comings and goings of his brothers and sisters. He didn't like living in a dormitory atmosphere with the other US amateur boxers. This was a part of the sport of boxing that he did not much like. But he understood that it was necessary.

In the ring at Las Vegas, the first Russian opponent he faced was at least six years older and far more experienced. Ray flattened him with a single left hook seconds into the fight. He was knocked down in his next bout, but got up before the count was over, and proceeded to get his revenge by knocking out his opponent in the third round.

After his strong showing against the Russians, Ray was being touted as a sure winner in the 1972 Eastern Olympic trials, which were held in Cincinnati, Ohio. Dave Jacobs went to Cincinnati with Ray, aware that Ray was still not old enough but wanting to see how far he could go. There, Tom 'Sarge' Johnson, an assistant coach on the Olympic Boxing Team, noticed Ray right away, and it is he who is credited with giving Ray the nickname 'Sugar'. One day, while watching Ray work out, Johnson turned to Dave Jacobs and remarked, 'That kid you got is sweet as sugar.' There is some question about when he made the remark – some say it was later, at the final trials in Fort Worth, Texas. But there is no question but that it was 'Sarge' Johnson who gave Ray the nickname he has carried ever since. Johnson died not long afterwards in a plane crash in Poland.

Ray won his initial bouts with ease, then advanced to the semi-finals. His opponent, Greg Whaley, was a native Cincinnatian, a hometown boy. Ray and Dave Jacobs had watched him fight earlier in the week, but when Ray entered the ring he really didn't know how he was going to fight Whaley. He decided to take a few minutes to feel out his opponent. But Whaley caught Ray early with some good punches, and Ray quickly reverted to his normal style, which was to use his speed to avoid punches and then counterpunch when the time was right. He realized that Whaley's punches hadn't hurt him, and he did more counterpunching than usual, landing several good hooks and rights.

When the bell rang to signal the end of the three-round bout, Ray stood in the ring waiting for the referee to grab his arm and raise it in victory. He was dumbfounded when the announcer said 'Whaley' rather than 'Leonard'. He walked around the ring in circles, dazed, as Dave Jacobs shouted protests at the judges and many in the crowd booed the decision. Only when Dave Jacobs entered the ring, threw his arm around Ray's shoulder, and led him back to the dressing-room did Ray begin to realize that he had lost. It was a new experience for him.

It was hard for a sixteen-year-old to understand politics, to have all sorts of people tell him he should have won, and yet to have the judges' original decision stand. He knew he had won the bout, other people knew he had won the bout, and yet there was no formal protest lodged. It was a lesson in reality for the kid. There was some poetic justice in the fact that Greg Whaley did not go beyond that semi-finals bout either. He was supposed to meet Norman Goins, a lightweight from Indianapolis, in the finals, but Ray had given him enough of a beating to sideline him. Whaley did not make the 1972 Olympics team. For Ray, there was one more chance to make the team – the final 'box-off' at Texas Christian University in Fort Worth where teams from the various armed services competed. Ray was invited to these final trials, and after much string-pulling (another lesson in the power of politics) he went to Fort Worth as a member of the army team.

He was under a great deal of strain. For a long time he had simply enjoyed boxing, with no real goals beyond winning the next fight. But the loss to Greg Whaley had hurt him psychologically, and when it dawned on him how much the people around him, like Dave Jacobs, had been counting on his winning, he began to feel as if he was somehow to blame. As he watched Jacobs and others scramble to get him on the army team, the idea that he ought to be in the Olympics struck him full force. He knew he had one more chance, and he believed that if he muffed it he would be letting down everyone who cared about him.

Ray got worried, so worried that he couldn't sleep at night or keep food down. But he kept pushing himself. The day before his last-chance fight he was running around a track at Texas Christian University when he collapsed from exhaustion. Dave Jacobs suddenly realized that the kid had been pushed too hard – months of constant competition in the Golden Gloves tournament, the AAU National Tournament, the meet against the Russian team in Las Vegas, the Eastern Olympics trials in Cincinnati – and all the while the pressure on him to make the Olympic boxing team had continued to build.

Now Jacobs made a decision with his young fighter in mind. He knew he could take Ray back to the locker room and let him rest awhile, hoping he would feel better and manage to compete the next day. He could also tell Ray right there that he was taking him out of the competition. But either course would mean hurting Ray's ego. So, Jacobs took Ray to the army team's doctor, and it was the doctor who disqualified Ray from the next day's competion, much to Jacobs' relief, and also, secretly, to Ray's.

The next day, Ray insisted that he felt fine and expressed anger at having been taken out of the competition. But Jacobs reminded him that in the end his opportunity to compete in the 1972 Olympics would probably have been taken away from him anyway, for he was still only sixteen and no matter how good a boxer he was the US Olympic team would not risk breaking an international Olympics rule when it came to major competition.

Ray went home, wiser and more experienced, and with a new nickname of which he was exceptionally proud. He intended to continue boxing, but he didn't have his heart set on making the 1976 Olympic boxing team until he watched the 1972 Olympics and saw Sugar Ray Seales win a gold medal. As he told Lawrence Linderman of *Playboy*, 'It suddenly dawned on me how close I'd come to going to the Olympics and how important it was to win a gold medal . . . I vowed that 1976 would be my year.'

2

The Drive to the Olympics

BOXING DID A lot for Sugar Ray Leonard: it gave him a confidence he had never known before, helped him develop self-discipline, and set up goals to work for. It gave him the chance to travel to cities he had only dreamed about seeing, and which he managed to appreciate in spite of his homesickness. It also made a great difference in his attitude towards school, for now fellow-students approached him to ask about his latest fight and he suddenly had something to say besides a quick 'Hi'. Although he became something of a celebrity in Palmer Park, he remained basically shy and unassuming, a loner with only a few close friends. He and Derrik Holmes had grown apart by then, and Derrik, who had shown some promise as a junior featherweight, later shot a man, as did another youngster who had started out with him in the Palmer Park Recreation Center boxing programme.

By the age of sixteen, however, Ray did have a girl-friend. Juanita Wilkinson, whom he called Nita, was a fellow-student at Parkdale High School who lived right around the corner from him. He had noticed her long before they were introduced by one of her girlfriends, but he had never summoned the courage to approach her himself. Once introduced, it took him some time to ask her out, but after the first date they became inseparable. They spent nearly every evening together, either at his house or hers. She accompanied him to the Recreation Center to watch him work out in the afternoons and at weekends and went to as many local competitions as she could, although she did not particularly enjoy them. At first, she had been somewhat enamoured of Ray's boxing celebrity, but once she saw him hit she began to feel differently. Although Ray nearly always won his fights, he did take his share of punches, and Nita hated to see him hit. She looked forward to the day when he would quit boxing, but she knew that he would not do so until he had won a gold medal at the 1976 Olympics.

This was now a firmly established goal for Ray. The US team had made such a poor showing in Munich that Ray was embarrassed for US boxing. Only one boxer, junior welterweight Ray Seales, had won a medal at the games, and officials of the AAU Boxing Commission determined to do better next time. They decided that US boxers needed more competitions, especially international competitions where they could gain a greater understanding and more experience of how foreign boxers fought, and the Commission pursued a far more energetic international competition schedule during the next four years.

Dave Jacobs and Sugar Ray Leonard agreed that US boxers needed more experience fighting against foreign opponents. Ray participated in as many international competitions as he could, and between whiles they studied as many films of foreign boxers as Jacobs could get hold of. Meanwhile, Ray competed in every local, regional and national competition, no matter how many bake sales they had to hold to pay the expenses.

In the beginning, Ray was so fired by his determination to win a gold medal in 1976 that he over-exerted himself, training as if the Olympics were four days, rather than four years, away. He trained so hard and competed so often that he hurt his hands, which were rather delicate for a fighter. Boxing several bouts in the space of a few days, as he did when he represented the United States against the Russian and East German teams that year, and when he competed in and won the Golden Gloves tournament, he asked more of his hands than they could take.

During the Golden Gloves tournament, they became swollen and sore. He tried all sorts of remedies, but nothing seemed to work. Dave Jacobs sought to protect Ray's knuckles with padding, but this was not allowed under amateur boxing rules. Only a thin strip of gauze could cover his knuckles, which was far short of the protection he needed, so he had to learn to live with the pain. In spite of the soreness and swelling he won his bouts, and attracted the attention of a number of people who believed he was wasting his talents as an amateur.

One, Baltimore boxing promoter Eli Hanover, sent Eddie Hrica, a well-known boxing 'matchmaker', to talk to Dave Jacobs about Ray's turning pro. Armed with a $5,000 cheque, made out to Ray, he hoped to seal the bargain immediately. But Hrica never got further in his negotiations than a brief meeting with Jacobs, who informed him flatly that Sugar Ray was not turning pro, at least not until after the Olympics.

To Ray, $5,000 was a lot of money, but he went along with Jacobs' decision because he trusted the older man's judgement, and because winning the Olympic gold medal was uppermost in his mind. It was a hard decision for Ray, who had once suffered from an inferiority complex because he was poor, but he had learned that being really good at something was an equally successful cure for inferiority as being well off. After all, he couldn't help the circumstances into which he was born, but he could do something about his own individual circumstances, and make something of himself.

Besides, Ray and Jacobs had already talked about the opportunities that would await him if he did win an Olympic gold medal. In the past, a gold medal had meant fame and fortune for the winner – big money for advertising sports equipment and healthy foods, personal appearances on television shows, jobs as colour commentators for TV sports broadcasts, sometimes even Hollywood film offers. To be sure, most of these champions were white, but Jacobs, for one, believed that Sugar Ray Leonard, with his baby face and charming grin, projected an image that would appeal to the American public. Ray was willing to wait for the financial rewards winning a gold medal might bring, rather than risk turning pro for $5,000 with no guarantee that he would ever make more than just that in the professional game.

Ray had other reasons for not wanting to turn pro. Although he didn't have a lot of experience with professional boxers, as a promising young amateur he'd already had his share of visits from has-beens who were still so tied to the game that they spent most of their time reminiscing about their days in boxing and trying to give advice to newcomers who showed promise. Too often, it seemed to Ray, these men were lonely and unhappy except when they were with other boxers and talking about fighting. And too often all they had to show for their boxing careers was physical injury – cauliflower ears and broken noses and failed brains. He did not want to end up like them, and early on he had determined that he was going to use boxing, not allow boxing to use him.

Ray was not yet seventeen years old when Nita announced that she was pregnant, and suddenly clouds loomed in Ray's bright future. He considered marrying her, and dropping out of school to get a job so he could support her and the child. But in his heart he knew he was not ready to be either a husband or a father. For her part, Juanita was frightened at the prospect of being an unmarried mother, but at the same time she was afraid to pressure Ray into a marriage and responsibilities he did not want, appreciating that she would surely lose him if she did so. For months, the two young people and their families agonized over what to do, and at length they all decided on a course that they hoped was the right one. Juanita would have the child and Ray would be the legal father of record, but they would not get married. Juanita would live at home. Above all the decision was Juanita's, and in making it she showed great compassion for the young man she loved, not to mention a sense of maturity beyond her years. She compared his dream and her dream and realized they could both come true if she did not demand all of her dream at once. Her dream was to marry Ray and have his child; she was having his child, but if she insisted on marrying she would deprive him of his dream of winning a gold medal at the Olympics. On the other hand, if she let him pursue his dream, she was certain that he would eventually marry her.

That summer, Ray Leonard accompanied the US amateur team on a month-long tour that took him to several countries in Europe and ended in the Soviet Union. It was his second trip abroad, the first having taken place in 1972, not long after he had failed to qualify for the Olympic boxing team. The AAU flew a team to Rome and from there drove the youths to a small village where a ring had been set up in the middle of a crowded street. Ray fought last, and knocked out his opponent in the second round. Until then, the crowd had been cheering noisily for the Italian fighter. Suddenly, all was quiet. Ray looked up to see a couple of hundred people closing in on the ring, and it occurred to him that they might attack him. But as the crowd reached the ring apron, they began to applaud, and a relieved Sugar Ray beamed in gratitude.

Back in Rome, Ray did some exploring around the mountainside church where the team was housed. He was inspecting a statue when he noticed a little girl staring at him. She turned and walked away, but a few minutes later she was back with two small friends. All three soon disappeared, and about fifteen minutes later Ray was startled to see about a hundred and fifty kids, led by a priest carrying a shepherd's crook, making their way up the mountain towards him. 'The kids surrounded me completely,' Ray told Lawrence Lindeman of *Playboy* in 1982, 'and while they were all whispering, this one little girl came up to me and touched my skin to see if the colour would rub off. I had an Afro then and a lot of the kids came up and felt my hair and then felt their own, and it really was funny. After that, they all sang a song to me and walked away. I really wish I could relive that, because it was a beautiful experience.'

Although Ray had looked forward to his second trip abroad and understood he needed the experience to prepare for the Olympics, he hated to leave Nita while she was pregnant. He fought well and won all his bouts, but he was homesick from the start, and he felt exceptionally uncomfortable in the Eastern European countries. At Warsaw airport, he was startled to see soldiers carrying sub-machine guns and actually pointing them at people.

He could not understand why there were curfews for ordinary citizens. He tried to call his mother, and learned that he had to sign up to make such a call a day in advance. When he did get through, he heard clicks on the line and was certain the phone was being tapped. Then, in mid-call, the line went dead and he was unable to re-establish the connection.

By the time Ray reached the Soviet Union he was feeling downright hopeless. He hated the food and was living almost entirely on ice-cream. Moreover, he was never more conscious of being black than he was in Russia, for the people stared at him and made him feel uncomfortable. They may have been simply curious, having been told constantly that blacks were subjected to extreme discrimination in the United States, but Ray reacted in a very different way to their curiosity from his reaction to the little children in Rome. At one point during his stay in the Soviet Union, Ray became so despondent that he got down on his knees and prayed to God that he would get through without losing his sanity. After that he felt better, and managed the rest of the trip without further incident.

Ray Leonard, Jr, was born 22 November 1973. Juanita dropped out of school to take care of him; later she made up the work she had missed and graduated. She remained at her parents' home while Ray continued to live with his parents. On the surface, his life did not change, but inside he was racked with guilt over forcing Juanita to carry such a heavy burden alone. He knew other young men who had made their girls pregnant and who had lived up to their responsibilities by dropping out of school and getting jobs. Suddenly, his intensive training seemed unimportant compared to the responsibilities of real life. Against the adult responsibility that Juanita had taken on, his goal of a gold medal seemed like a kid's dream. For a time, although the road to the Olympics was unobstructed for him, he lost his sense of determination to reach the end of that road. He began to resent his gruelling training regimen. He had trouble concentrating on bouts. It is difficult to measure the effects of an athlete's mental state in competition, and it is hard to know just what will adversely affect his or her mental state. There are times when an athlete can be going through the worst possible emotional problems and still perform at peak, and there are also times when seemingly minor personal difficulties will severely hurt athletic performance. Neither the athlete nor the outside observer can pinpoint the effects exactly, but it is surely no coincidence that in the year after his son was born out of wedlock Sugar Ray Leonard lost some important fights.

At least one of these fights was a clear-cut loss. In the 1974 national AAU finals, Ray lost to Randy Shields because in that bout at least Shields was the better fighter. The other two losses were against foreign opponents in foreign countries, and both decisions were highly controversial.

Against Russian champion Anatoli Kamnev, Sugar Ray fought so well that when the judges awarded the win to Kamnev, the largely Russian audience started to whistle. Ray, who didn't know what that meant, soon learned that it was the European way of booing. Kamnev himself walked across the ring and gave Ray the trophy that had just been presented to him. Still, on the record books, it went down as a loss by Leonard.

During that same European tour by the US amateur team, Sugar Ray lost by decision to a Polish fighter, Kazimier Szczerba, despite the fact that he knocked Szczerba down three times in the final round and in the opinion of most observers knocked him out the third time. The Polish referee, however, ruled that the third knockdown had occurred after the match-ending bell had sounded. Szczerba had to be literally held up by his trainers as he received the victor's trophy, but another decision went down against Sugar Ray Leonard in the record books. It was the fifth and last loss of his amateur career.

Such close 'political' losses did not help Ray Leonard's attitude toward boxing, which grew worse as 1974 progressed. Many times he came close to hanging up his gloves, but each time he was talked out of it. His brother Roger, who had enlisted in the Air Force and was distinguishing himself in military boxing competition, his father, and everyone at the Palmer Park Recreation Center urged him to continue. One of the most persistent in keeping him on the Olympic gold track was Janks Morton, assistant boxing trainer at the Center and a former pro football player who was convinced that Ray had the talent to go all the way if he could only regain his concentration and fighting spirit. Morton harped on how tragic it would be for Ray to throw away years of strict training, and gradually Ray saw that Morton made sense. He really could not turn back now. The old determination to win eventually returned, but he was equally certain that once he won the gold medal he would quit boxing. He wanted to go to college and major in communications, and eventually he wanted a career in television. Through boxing, he had learned that he enjoyed being in the spotlight and that there was a lot of natural 'ham' in him when he was the centre of attention. People responded to him, and in turn he grew even more responsive to his audiences. He knew he could communicate, and a career in communications seemed the natural choice for him.

Training became easier for him once he had determined why he was doing it, but for Ray and the other young boxers who worked out at the Palmer Park Recreation Center, conditions were still primitive. The Center had yet to acquire a real boxing ring, and Ray continued to spar inside taped boundaries. During the summer of 1975 the Center sponsored a special basketball programme, and Ray's time to train for the annual Pan American Games was curtailed. Hardly would he get warmed up when Director Ollie Dunlap would sadly inform him and Dave Jacobs that the basketball players needed the whole court, which included the 'boxing ring', and that they would have to vacate it. Nevertheless, Sugar Ray was a champion at the Pan American Games.

By 1975, Olympics excitement was palpable in US amateur boxing. AAU Boxing Commission officials were pleased with the young talent being groomed, and they stepped up their efforts to give the youngsters as much experience in foreign competition as possible. Between 1972 and 1976 US amateur boxers competed against foreign teams some 50 times, including 33 times overseas. No single boxer competed in more than 10 or 15 matches, for AAU officials didn't want the foreign teams to learn how much talent there was in US amateur boxing. There was a lot of fine talent. In addition to the two Leonard brothers, Sugar Ray and Roger, there were two Spinks brothers, Leon and Michael, and then there were a number of individuals, among them Howard Davis. These young men were almost certain to win in the Olympic trials and make the team.

Sadly, Roger Leonard did not. His best fighting weight was 139 pounds, which put him in the AAU light-welterweight class. That was also Sugar Ray's class, and Roger did not want to compete against his brother. So, he put on more weight and competed in the next higher class, the 147-pound welterweight, where he lost in the semi-finals.

By late May 1976 the US Olympic boxing team had been selected, and with his team-mates, who included Howard Davis and the Spinks brothers, Ray travelled to Burlington, Vermont, for a month of intensive training. US Olympic team coaches now took over from Dave Jacobs and Janks Morton, who stayed behind in Palmer Park, and Ray missed them sorely, just as he missed his family. From Burlington, the team went directly to Montreal, so Ray was away for nearly two months, his longest stretch ever away from home. To stave off homesickness, he armed himself with pictures of his family, including photos of Nita and Ray, Jr, in various sizes.

No one but Sugar Ray and his friends and family back home knew how homesick he was. To his team-mates and coaches, and to Olympic officials, he seemed a quiet, confident young man, easy to get along with. The US press found him especially attractive, and the veteran sportscaster Howard Cosell, who had been almost alone in supporting Muhammad Ali during the time when he had refused induction into the army on the basis of his religious beliefs, developed a keen interest in him. In his 'prettiness', and in his speed and quick reflexes, young Sugar Ray Leonard reminded Cosell of Ali in his younger, Cassius Clay, days, and Cosell talked of Ray at every opportunity as the kind of fighter that boxing sorely needed.

Other reporters were drawn to him as well. His boyish face and big smile were photogenic, his on-camera presence sparkling, his ability to relax during interviews impressive in one so young. He was soon the 'darling' of the American team, the essence of the clean-cut all-American kid, in spite of the fact that it was common knowledge that he had fathered a child out of wedlock. Sugar Ray was so matter-of-fact about it, and so clearly proud of Juanita and Ray, Jr, tiny pictures of whom he wore pinned to his boxing socks, that reporters saw no reason to play up this flaw in his otherwise nearly perfect image.

Ray saw competition early in the games; his first bout took place on the first full day of competition and he was excused from participating in the long march to open the games by the president of the US team so he could conserve his strength. His opponent in that first match was a Swede, Ulf Carlsson, and Ray took the three-round bout easily, controlling it all the way. He danced and feinted, smiled often at his opponent, and seemed to take the opportunity to display every aspect of the crowd-pleasing ring personality that had been compared not only to Ali's but also to that of Sugar Ray Robinson and Kid Gavilan.

Gavilan, the welterweight of the 1940s, had been famous for his 'bolo' punches, uppercuts that start from behind the body, with the arm wound up as if to throw a baseball. Ray had realized early on that such a move confused his opponents and gave him a psychological edge, so he used it on occasion to considerable advantage. Sugar Ray Robinson was famous in his heyday for his lightning-quick combination of lefts and rights, and Ray's combinations were his best shots. Muhammad Ali was known for any number of ring tactics, among them the 'Ali

Shuffle', in which he danced around th
arms dangling at his sides, and his i
opponents) way of jutting out his chin as
punch. Sugar Ray Leonard used all these
combining them with a few of his own, such
brilliant smile at his opponent after being hit,
'Ah, that didn't hurt.'

At times during the past couple of years had deliberately refrained from these tactics, for although he firmly believed that a crucial part of ring skill was to 'psych' opponents, he also understood that some people resented these techniques as 'hotdogging'. Foreign judges particularly took a dim view of these tactics, and after his two 1974 losses to Polish boxer Kazimier Szczerba and Russian Anatoli Kamnev, some American boxing officials had suggested that the judges' decisions might have had something to do with his showboating tactics. From then on, Sugar Ray had fought straight up whenever he was in a potentially unfriendly arena, but in Montreal in 1976 the atmosphere was pro-American, and Ray decided to fight the way he liked best. He had worked long and hard to get to Montreal, and since he planned to quit boxing after the Olympics, he saw no reason not to go out in style.

His next opponent was a Russian named Valery Limasov, an experienced left-hander who had won many bouts by virtue of the unorthodox style that marks southpaw fighters, a style that often confounded right-handed opponents. Sugar Ray, however, did not lose his timing or his balance, and had no trouble landing some hard punches. But Limasov stayed in the match through the entire three rounds, winning the respect of the crowd, if not the fight. When Ray was announced as the winner, he stepped to the centre of the ring and unfurled the flag of Prince Georges County, Maryland, where Palmer Park is located. It was a move calculated to inspire the folks back home, and it did even more for the image of Sugar Ray Leonard in the eyes of American reporters and the general public. Black athletes at the Olympics had not always displayed such patriotism; back in 1968, some black

.es had refused to participate in the Olympics .ogether, and two black medal winners had raised clenched fists at the playing of the national anthem, shocking their fellows back home, as they intended. With his patriotic gesture, Sugar Ray did much to soften that memory.

Ray's third opponent was Clinton McKenzie of England, a favourite of the crowd, which included many Canadians of English descent. In retrospect, Ray made a mistake using his showboating techniques against this particular opponent. While he scored at the end of the first round with a flurry of combinations, landed both solid right jabs and left hooks in the second, and scored with another series of combinations in the third, overall he had done less punching than feinting, shuffling, smiling and dancing, which didn't sit well with the crowd. They booed Ray during the match, and it was not a sound he was accustomed to hearing from his audiences. While in the end they cheered his victory, he remembered the boos more than the cheers.

Three opponents down, three to go. Each time he finished a fight, Ray felt a great let-down, greater than after a bout close to home. While there was always some 'decompression' involved after all the self-psyching and physical exertion of a match, at least when he fought near his own community he could then go home to family and friends. Here in Montreal, all he could do was telephone home. None of his friends or family was in Montreal because they couldn't afford the travel expenses; and also, there were so many fighters from so many countries engaging in so many contests, Ray's fights were spread out; he had already been in Montreal over a week, and he'd fought just three times.

It was a strange time for the Olympic athletes in Montreal; an uneasiness pervaded the Olympic Village. Back in 1972 in Munich, Palestinian terrorists had broken into the Olympic Village and killed several members of the Israeli Olympic team. To ensure that a similar tragedy did not occur in Montreal, there was exceptionally tight security at the Olympic Village, with an army of guards constantly patrolling and checking identity cards. Although Ray understood the reason, he felt uncomfortable in that atmosphere and missed home even more. He spent much of his free time gazing at photographs of Juanita and Little Ray and telling himself that if he could just keep himself up mentally, and if his hands would just hold out, the ordeal would be over in a few days. He would have his long-sought gold medal and could start living a normal life.

In the quarter-finals, Ray beat Ulrich Beyer of East Germany and advanced to the semi-finals, where, he learned, he would face Kazimier Szczerba, the Polish fighter who had won the disputed decision back in 1974. He had no trouble psyching himself up for this bout, but his hands, especially his right knuckles, were bothering him, and no amount of ice packs, soaking in Epsom Salts, or applications of Ben Gay did much to relieve either the swelling or the pain. Thus, when he met Szczerba, he consciously favoured his right hand, concentrating on left jabs and hooks. Even holding back this way, he beat Szczerba. In fact, so there would be no opportunity this time for the decision to go the other way, he KO'd the guy.

Sugar Ray called home after his victory, and was dejected when he could not get an answer either at his own home or at Juanita's. Everyone knew he was fighting that day, and he wondered if they just didn't care. Here he was, subjecting himself to abuse, endangering his hands, homesick after having been away for more than a month, and back in Palmer Park the people who were supposed to be in his corner were going about business as usual. He had no way of knowing that his loved ones were at that moment on their way to Montreal.

Dave Jacobs had planned all along to fly up to Montreal for Ray's last couple of fights, but as the time approached he realized he couldn't leave Ray's family behind. Neither the Leonards nor Juanita could afford the plane fare to Montreal, so Jacobs decided to take them all, by van. The Leonards were delighted with the idea, and when he learned that his boss would not pay him for the days he took off to go to Montreal Cicero Leonard threw his usual financial caution to the winds and informed his employer that he was going anyway. The opportunity to see his son win an Olympic gold medal was worth the loss of a few days' pay.

A van designed to hold six people accommodated ten for the trip: Jacobs, Cicero and Getha Leonard, Roger, who was home on leave from the Air Force, Juanita, Little Ray, Ray's two younger sisters, Sharon and Sandy, and two of Ray's friends. They covered the side windows of the van with pictures of Ray and placed a sign on the back that read:

WE'VE COME A LONG WAY TO SEE
SUGAR RAY WIN THE GOLD MEDAL – ALL THE
WAY FROM PALMER PARK, MD.,
PRINCE GEORGES COUNTY, U.S.A.

The fourteen-hour trip to Montreal was a long, tiring drive for the group, who dubbed themselves the sardines and Jacobs 'King Sardine'. They drove all night and took a couple of wrong turns along the way, but the following morning, tired but triumphant, they arrived at the Olympic Village. Ray had awakened and was getting ready to go out and run when he learned that his family was there. He had never been happier in his life.

The men decided to spend the next couple of nights in the van, parked in a lot across from the boxing arena. The women were able to find a room in a nearby motel. All spent their days at the van, which with its proud signs became something of an attraction for other visitors to the Olympics. Some of these visitors helped secure tickets to Sugar Ray's title bout, and on the night of the biggest fight of his life his personal fan club was in the VIP section, cheering him on.

Andres Aldama, Ray's final opponent, was a Cuban known for his powerful punches, especially his left hook, who had won his previous five Olympic bouts even more easily than Ray had won his. The US boxing team coaches had studied his style closely and concluded that Ray's habit of dancing and feinting might play into the hands of his opponent, who would find it easier to unleash his left hook against an opponent who favoured the outside. They suggested that Ray should go inside on Aldama, denying him the room for his powerful punch. When the opening bell sounded, Ray went on the attack immediately, and while Aldama refused to give any ground he was clearly hampered and unable to fight in his usual style. In the second round, Ray kept up his charge and forced Aldama to step back as he unleashed one of his lightning-quick combinations. Perhaps confused by the blows, Aldama misread the referee's motion about a minute later as the two fighters clutched each other. Thinking that the referee had signalled them to break apart, he hesitated for just an instant, and that was enough time for Ray to seize his opportunity and land a solid left hook to the chin, driving Aldama down on one knee. The referee counted eight before the Cuban got back to his feet.

Clearly worried, Aldama came out in the third round looking for a knockout. But Ray had the psychological advantage now, and he used it, easily ducking Aldama's wild punches and unloading a five-punch flurry to the head that forced his opponent to take a standing eight-count. Again Ray attacked, knocking Aldama down, and again Aldama had to take the required count of eight. When the final bell rang, there was no question that Sugar Ray Leonard was the victor, in one of the most decisive wins of his career. The Olympic gold medal was his.

Amid wild cheering, sportscaster Howard Cosell, who had been covering the fight at ringside for television, pushed his way up to Ray. Cosell had predicted the popularity of Sugar Ray Leonard at the Olympics before the games had even started, and now he told TV viewers that Ray Leonard would be a rich and great fighter once he turned professional. But Ray shook his head. 'I've fought my last fight,' he said. 'My journey has ended. My dream is fulfilled.'

He was not, however, feeling very fulfilled at that

moment. In fact, he was not feeling anything at all. Almost in a daze, he bent to receive the gold medal hung around his neck. Then, amid cheers, he walked alone out of the arena. His family and friends looked in vain for him until at last they found him out in the parking lot, sitting in the van. He wanted to go home, he said. He didn't even want to take the time to return to the Olympics Village to claim his belongings. He wanted to go home *now.*

3

Sugar Ray Turns Pro

THE VAN ATTRACTED considerable attention as it made its way back to Palmer Park from Montreal. Although the US Olympic boxing team as a whole had done exceptionally well – others, including Leon and Michael Spinks, had also won gold medals – it was Sugar Ray who had really captured the public's imagination. The border guard at the St Lawrence Seaway wanted to touch the medal – and kiss Getha Leonard. Fellow-motorists honked their horns, gas station attendants wanted to shake Ray's hand. When the van reached the outskirts of Palmer Park, a police escort was waiting to accompany the hometown hero to the biggest welcome any resident had ever received.

During the next few days, the Leonards were besieged by telephone calls and visits from well-wishers, friends and strangers alike. Reporters showed up for interviews at all hours, photographers pressed for 'one more picture'. County officials came to call; mail from all over the world began to arrive, delivered by the Post Office in large cloth bags. Everyone wanted to know why Ray wasn't going to turn pro. He had the talent, he had the fame. If he turned pro, he could make a lot of money.

But Ray's mind was made up. After an amateur career of 170 fights, and a record of 165 wins and five losses, he was quitting boxing and going to school. Muhammad Ali, who was still his boxing idol, said that young athletes, no matter how good they were, should get an education first. The odds were always against a young athlete making it in professional sports, but were always on the side of a young person with a good education. Ray had taken that advice to heart. Despite his busy boxing schedule, he had managed to graduate from high school and had been offered a congressional scholarship to the University of Maryland. In another two months he would be a college student, majoring in communications as he had hoped. He also had plans to do something in the recreational field, helping poor kids to become somebody through athletics. Meanwhile, of course, he had every intention of taking advantage of any opportunities for public appearances and product endorsements that he was certain would come as a result of his Olympic victory. He imagined his picture on the Wheaties box, which traditionally featured the latest American athletic star. Then, just days after his return, Sugar Ray Leonard was the subject of headlines for which he had not bargained. Sugar Ray Leonard, Olympic hero, had been named in a paternity suit.

The suit came about because Juanita had applied for public assistance without telling Ray or his parents. Knowing how hard Ray was training for the Olympics, she had not wanted to upset him, but having a small child was proving too expensive for her to handle without help. The doctor's bills, food, clothes, shoes, toys and all the other things she felt Little Ray needed were beyond her father's budget. She knew Ray did not have any money. Nor did she feel she could ask the elder Leonards, who despite the fact that some of the older children were now self-supporting, were still not in a position to give much financial help. Cicero Leonard was ailing. He had spinal pneumonia and tuberculosis simultaneously, had missed a lot of time at work, but kept on working as much as he was able to in order to support his family. So, while Ray was in Montreal, Juanita applied for food stamps, having no idea what would happen as a result.

Since 1975 and the passage of a new Maryland law aimed at curbing welfare cheating, it had been standard procedure for welfare authorities to initiate a paternity suit when an unmarried mother applied for public assistance. Such a suit was required as part of the proof that the woman was eligible for help, but while Juanita dutifully filled out the requisite forms she really did not understand the procedure. She certainly did not expect the press to find out about it. But someone in the state welfare department must have leaked the story to the Washington *Star*, and the story was a headline item the following day.

Although the story did include the information that the suit was a formality, necessary whether or not Ray Leonard acknowledged being the father of Juanita Wilkinson's child, it was the headline that people remembered: SUGAR RAY'S PATERNITY SUIT. Ray was furious when he saw that headline. He was angry with Juanita for not telling him she had applied for food stamps, but he was especially angry with the press and the welfare people for choosing this particular time to air as a scandal a matter that he considered to be a personal problem and not public business. Although he had never made a secret of Little Ray's birth out of wedlock, he certainly did not want it emblazoned in headlines. He thought about the hundreds of kids who looked up to him and cringed when he realized that he had set a lousy example as someone who shirked his responsibilities.

Juanita was far more upset than Ray was, for she felt responsible for bringing down adverse publicity on Ray and his family, not to mention her guilt about applying for welfare without telling the Leonards. The Leonards, too, were embarrassed by the publicity, and especially by the implication that they were too poor to help support their son's child. But somehow they all managed to get through the crisis, and perhaps to emerge more close as a family than before. Juanita should have come to them first. They would see that she got the assistance she needed, no matter how much of a financial burden it would place upon them.

In general, the public were supportive of Sugar Ray. He received plenty of hate mail, but he also received letters from people who thought the Washington *Star* story had been unfair. The *Star* heard from the public as well, and an official of the paper publicly admitted that the story had been over-sensationalized. The damage, however, had already been done. It is impossible to guess how many product-endorsement offers might have come Ray Leonard's way, how many chances to do television commercials at hefty fees, if not for the highly publicized paternity suit against him. Whether the publicity affected his chances adversely or not, there were no offers to benefit financially from his Olympic fame.

There were plenty of big-sounding schemes pitched to Ray at that time, schemes that promised to make him a lot of money. Whenever he expressed interest, the schemers promised to get back to him with details. While he waited for those details, he started accepting invitations to appear for free at scores of gyms and recreation centres and schools. He had always been willing to make such appearances, but now it was especially important to him to show young people that he was not a shirker of responsibilities, that by his work and effort during the past four years he could be a role model for young people.

Ray was kept so busy making personal appearances over the next couple of months that he had little time to think about what he was going to do for the rest of his life. At least, he excused his refusal to think about the future by citing his commitments. Actually, he was deeply confused. He still was not supporting Juanita and Little Ray, and he didn't think he could go off to the University of Maryland for four years and leave her to fend for herself. He kept waiting for the proposers of all those schemes to get back to him, but they did not seem to be in any hurry. He still hadn't been offered any major commercial endorsements and was beginning to accept one of the realities of his life: he was not Mark Spitz or Bruce Jenner, two white Olympic gold medallists who had made millions doing product-endorsements. Whites were in the majority in the United States, whites bought the majority of consumer products, and white athletes untainted by scandal were the ones who were sought by product advertisers. Ray was black and an unmarried father who had been the subject of a much publicized paternity suit, hardly a marketable commodity for marketing commodities. Within a month after his return from Montreal he also discovered, to his sad surprise, that people were already forgetting the Olympics.

At the time he was accompanying Janks Morton, whose steady job was selling insurance, on his rounds a couple of days a week. They would arrive at a prospective client's house and Morton would proudly introduce Sugar Ray Leonard; often the client's face would take on a blank look no matter how hard he or she tried to summon a smile of recognition. Ray began to know how fleeting fame could be, and he did not like to see the spotlight slipping away.

In late September, Ray did get an offer that he knew was real when he and Morton were invited to New York to see the heavyweight title bout between Muhammad Ali and Ken Norton. King wasted little time offering him a big-money pro contract, which, on close reading, contained so many options in King's favour that Ray would be practically owned by King. Around the same time, Muhammad Ali gave Ray some timely advice: if you decide to turn pro, don't sign your life away. Don't make the same mistake I made.

There were other offers for Ray to turn pro, but the last thing he wanted was to be 'owned' by anyone else. For that matter, he didn't even want to be a pro fighter. But he had decided not to take the congressional scholarship to the University of Maryland because it did not include money for day-to-day living. What he needed was work that paid enough for him to support Juanita. For the time being, he took a part-time job at the Palmer Park Recreation Center. He turned his first paycheck over to Juanita, who cashed it and then carefully placed the stub between the pages of her Bible. More than a decade later, Ray discovered it there, and chuckled when he saw the amount – $185.00 for two weeks' work.

Meanwhile, Janks Morton was getting worried about Ray's inability to make a decision about turning pro, for Morton knew that Ray did not have all the time in the world in which to make it. Morton had seen the blank looks on his clients' faces when he had introduced them to Sugar Ray, and he knew that even boxing people would not stay excited about him for ever. If Ray waited too long, he'd be the youngest has-been in boxing history. Right now, he was in top physical condition, and his mind and heart, though confused and troubled, were still in the habit of focusing with determination on a single goal. But if he waited much longer, not only would his physical condition deteriorate, so would his concentration. Morton decided that someone ought to step in and give Ray some direction, not to push him into anything, but to give him a clear idea of his options and the consequences of each, to bring some order into his life. Morton was also smart enough to realize that no one who was close to Ray would be able to do that successfully. Ray was far too sensitive at that time to take advice from his friends and family, but Morton reasoned that he might listen to an objective outsider.

Morton arranged for Ray to meet Charles Brotman, a public relations man whom he knew. Brotman was careful not to give Ray the impression that he wanted to run his life for him, but rather suggested that one who made so many public appearances would benefit from organized scheduling. Ray liked Brotman, and soon presented the man with a stack of napkins, restaurant receipts and sundry other slips of paper on which he had made hasty notes about places he was supposed to visit and business deals in which he was supposed to be involved. Brotman sorted through the papers and set up a schedule of appearances that would enable Ray to keep his commitments without running madly from one commitment to another. He made calls and arranged for the payment of a fee in cases where it was appropriate. He also followed up the various business deals that had been proposed to Ray. Occasionally, he mentioned to Ray the pros and cons of various possible life courses, but he never preached, and for that Ray was grateful.

In the end, Ray made the decision to turn pro not because it was a course he wanted to take but because it was thrust upon him. He had known for a while that his father was in poor health, although the older man kept on working and didn't complain. Years later, Ray told an interviewer from *Ebony* magazine, 'He never, not once, showed the pain he was feeling. He just kept right on working to support the family, kept working so I could get to the Olympics. For fourteen years he worked in a supermarket. The courage he displayed in the face of that kind of adversity, that's what it means to be a man, and it's something you never forget.' But when Ray's mother suffered a heart attack and was forced to quit her job, the Leonards suddenly faced the deepest financial trouble they had ever known, and Ray knew that he no longer had the luxury of sitting around and wondering what to do with his life. Of the Leonard children, he was the only one in a potential position to make enough money to support his parents and younger sisters. And then there were Juanita and Ray, Jr, to think about – he could no longer expect his parents to help out there. So, he would continue fighting, and his goal would not be just to make money but to do something really big, something special.

Once he had made the decision to turn pro, Ray realized that he hadn't the foggiest notion how to go about it. If he could possibly help it, he did not want to sign with Don King or any other promoter who would take more than he gave. But he knew he had to have people to represent him in lining up fights, promoting them, handling the legal matters of contracts. He also needed money to pay those people, for gym fees, for equipment, travel expenses, for the various fees required by the boxing organizations in order to be certified a professional. When he told his friends and family that he had decided to turn pro, he also confessed that he didn't know what the next step was.

Janks Morton had some ideas, however. He was no professional boxing insider, but he did know that Ray would need a good lawyer. He immediately took Ray to see Mike Trainer, a lawyer in Silver Springs, Maryland, who happened to play on his local softball team. At first Ray felt uncomfortable with Trainer, who was white, for he felt as if he had to place his life in Trainer's hands. But Morton assured him that Trainer could be trusted, and since Trainer was willing to work without fee Ray had little choice. An unpaid lawyer was the only kind he could afford. For his part, Trainer took on the job because he enjoyed the challenge and the chance to learn about a completely new area. He also had some ideas about the fight business that were entirely new.

Thus began one of the most remarkable relationships in boxing, if not in the sports world as a whole. If Sugar Ray

Leonard is sometimes accused of approaching the game like an accountant, it is largely due to Trainer's influence. From the outset, he emphasized independence, and he treated Ray's career like a corporation. He knew enough about the traditional fight game to know that the majority of fighters were exploited, their hard-won earning treated as spoils to be divided among greedy managers and promoters. As Trainer once put it, 'That's not fair. I'm a lawyer. I believe in equity. Most of those guys are hustlers. They believe in nothing.'

Raising money was the first priority and there were plenty of people around who were eager to finance Sugar Ray Leonard's pro career. But Ray made it clear to Trainer at the outset that he didn't want to be beholden to any one backer. Long before Muhammad Ali had cautioned him not to sign his life away, it had bothered him to hear professional fight managers talk about 'my fighter' or 'my boy'. So, Trainer sought a group of investors to back Ray. In this way, he reasoned, no one investor could exercise undue influence.

As soon as word got out that Ray was turning pro, Trainer was besieged by offers of financial backing – so many, in fact, that he decided to hold a public meeting of all prospective backers. At the meeting, it quickly became clear that many of these potential investors wanted Ray to do more than just box in return for their investment. A store manager want him to spend one day a week at his place of business; a jewellery salesman wanted Ray to go out on the road with him twice a week. At that rate, Ray wouldn't even have time to train. Trainer politely thanked them for coming and adjourned the meeting.

Puzzling over how to get the money Ray needed without lots of strings attached, Trainer considered applying for a bank loan, which was the way he had financed his own law school education. But the bank officers he approached did not think much of a boxer's promising future as loan collateral, and turned Trainer down. At last, Trainer decided to go to his own friends and clients and raise about $20,000 from them. He had no idea of Ray's potential to earn money as a pro fighter and had essentially picked the sum of $20,000 out of a hat. He didn't know if that was enough of a stake to launch the career of a professional fighter, but it sounded like a sum he could raise. After making dozens of calls, he rounded up twenty-four people, each of whom agreed to loan Ray $1,000 or less for four years at eight per cent interest. (Trainer also picked the term of four years out of a hat, having no idea what Ray might be able to win in four years, assuming he won anything.) Among them, they put up a total of $21,000, with the promise of nothing in return but their original investment plus interest, *if* Ray succeeded as a professional. If he did not, then they faced losing their investment. It was to Mike Trainer's credit that these two dozen small investors trusted him enough to take the gamble; it was also to his credit that he was willing to stake his reputation with his friends on a young kid who would barely look him in the eye. He did tell Ray that it might be necessary for him to take a part-time job at some point, because the investors were his friends and ought to be paid back if at all possible.

Trainer made it clear to all the investors that no one owned a 'piece' of Sugar Ray Leonard, and to make that position even stronger he drew up papers creating a corporation called Sugar Ray Leonard, Inc., with Ray himself as the only stockholder. He then signed Ray to a personal services contract with the corporation, at a salary of $475.00 a week, at which rate, of course, the $21,000 wouldn't even last a year. Trainer appreciated, however, that Ray needed to feel financially secure and that he would not be able to concentrate on boxing if he was not. With a steady salary, Ray could help both his families and feel as if he were living up to his responsibilities.

The next step was to start building an organization, and Ray wanted Dave Jacobs and Janks Morton. He also wanted Mike Trainer, who agreed to stay on and handle business and legal matters at an hourly fee. None of them knew much about the world of professional boxing, and all agreed that the organization had to include at least one person who knew that world intimately. Charles Brotman was still helping Ray with his personal appearance scheduling, and he was now asked to find a knowledgeable manager for Ray. Brotman, too, was a stranger to the boxing world, but he did know whom to call. He compiled a list of names, and Trainer, Brotman, Jacobs, Morton and Ray began meeting various men. These included Eddie Futch and Gil Clancy, two respected manager/trainers in the fight game, but the man they eventually decided upon was the man whom Muhammad Ali had recommended – Angelo Dundee.

Dundee didn't ask Ray to move to another city, as most of the others did, citing the fact that in a bigger city, like New York or Philadelphia, where there was a bigger fight market and more media coverage, a new fighter would have greater opportunities. Ray, who got homesick even on short trips, didn't want to be away from his family for more than a few days at a time. Dundee said that his personal philosophy was: 'It costs nothing to be nice,' and Ray liked that. He also liked the idea that Dundee had trained Muhammad Ali since the days when he was Cassius Clay, and was still acting as his cornerman. Moreover, Ray decided that Dundee's wife, Helen, reminded him of his mother.

Angelo Dundee was famous in the boxing world for having trained Ali, but he had trained many others, including seven other champions. He had been the cornerman for Carmen Basilio, who won both the welterweight and middleweight titles, the trainer-manager of Willie Pastrano, the light-heavyweight champion from 1963 to 1965, whom Dundee had started training in 1952 when Pastrano was sixteen. He had never been a fighter himself. In boxing since 1948, he had learned the game from the gym level up, training fighters of every weight class and level of talent. He'd been educated in the tricks of the trade by some of the cleverest managers in the history of the game, and although he had had plenty of experience in the smoke-filled rooms with the not-so-sterling characters who made not-quite-legal deals, he had a reputation as a straight-shooter. And in a world where making enemies was a fact of life, there was hardly a man who didn't like Angelo Dundee.

There was no question that Dundee knew boxing, and he had the experience and connections to line up the right opponents for Sugar Ray. He knew just about every fighter, trainer and manager personally, and he could find out quickly about anyone else. He was as comfortable in Latin-American boxing circles as in North American ones, for he spoke Spanish and had trained Cuban fighters before the 1956 revolution that had brought Fidel Castro to power. Moreover, he quickly demonstrated his ability to devise unusual solutions to problems in training, solving the problem of Ray's sensitive hands, which could be hurt even on punching bags. When Ray trained, Dundee wrapped his hands in women's sanitary towels. Although Ray was embarrassed at first, he decided that he would be a fool not to use whatever worked.

Importantly, for Sugar Ray at that time, Dundee was quite willing to take less than the usual 30 per cent manager's cut. While serving officially as manager, he would not actually deal with Ray on a day-to-day basis. Instead, he would line up opponents for Ray, help promote his fights, oversee arrangements, and only get personally involved in Ray's training in the last couple of weeks of pre-fight training. In return, he would be paid 15 per cent of Ray's earnings.

With his organization complete, it was time for Ray's début as a professional boxer. Dundee wanted an opponent who would be a challenge to Ray, but not too big a challenge, for it would not do for Ray to lose his first professional fight. On the other hand, it would also not do for Ray to fight a stiff, a talentless fighter whom he could beat too easily. The point of the first fight, Dundee explained, was to show the boxing world that Ray could carry the potential he'd had as an amateur into the pro game. Plenty of talented amateurs had failed to make this transition.

Eddie Hrica, the matchmaker Dundee contacted, offered him a choice of four possible opponents, from among whom Dundee chose Luis (the Bull) Vega, a stocky young fighter out of Reading, Pennsylvania, whose record was 14 wins (3 knockouts) and 8 losses. Vega was tough and had never been knocked off his feet, but in Dundee's opinion, if Ray had what it took to be a pro he would beat him.

4

To the Championship, One Step at a Time

AS SOON AS Sugar Ray Leonard announced his intention to turn pro, officials of the city of Baltimore had let it be known that they would like him to fight his first pro bout in their city. The commissioner of the city's Civic Center pledged money towards the purse, and CBS-TV matched that sum in return for the right to broadcast the match. After announcing that he was turning pro, Ray had been offered a contract as a boxing analyst with the network, and in January 1977 he worked ringside for the first time when his Olympic team-mates Howard Davis and Leon Spinks made their professional débuts. After that, he concentrated on his own professional début the following month.

In preparation for the Vega fight Ray ran and sparred and studied videotapes to analyse his opponent's style, but he spent as much time promoting the fight as he did training for it. In fact, everyone connected with Sugar Ray Leonard, Inc., worked night and day to publicize his first pro match, for in the modern fight game an athlete must be 'marketable' or he may as well get into another line of work. Ray had to attract a lot of attention and a big audience if he wanted a large purse and good media coverage. If a lot of people attended the fight, or watched it on television, he could point to attendance figures and ratings when negotiating for his next fight. In a promotional plan worked out by Brotman and Trainer, the fight was advertised on billboards, posters and the backs of buses; the press and public were invited to watch Ray work out; press releases were sent to all the out-of-town newspapers and radio and television stations. Sugar Ray even sent President Jimmy Carter a telegram, inviting him to attend the fight:

> I RESPECTFULLY INVITE YOU AND YOUR FAMILY TO BE PRESENT AT MY PROFESSIONAL DEBUT IN BALTIMORE, SATURDAY, FEB. 5 AT 4:30 P.M.
> THIS WILL BE MY FIRST BOUT SINCE WINNING THE OLYMPIC GOLD MEDAL AT MONTREAL. IF YOU ARE UNABLE TO ATTEND, PLEASE TUNE IN CBS TELEVISION.
> WITH GREAT EXPECTATIONS
>
> SINCERELY,
>
> SUGAR RAY LEONARD

Of course, neither Ray nor any of his advisers had any expectation at all that the President would attend the fight, but they did expect the press, to whom they distributed copies of the telegram, to pick up on the story, and they were right. It was an unusual angle, almost guaranteed to get results.

On the day before his pro début, Sugar Ray took Little Ray to see the movie *Rocky.* The next afternoon, the movie still fresh in his mind, he entered the ring at Baltimore's Civic Center wearing a purple robe he had designed himself. The crowd in the arena numbered 10,270, more than had ever come to a fight there before, even to an Ali exhibition bout. They went wild when Ray arrived, and he smiled, feeling confident, though a glance at the scowling Luis Vega, who looked as tough as his reputation, quickly reminded him that this was no movie. This was the real thing, and all his dreams, not to mention other people's money, were on the line.

The six-round fight began slowly. Sugar Ray danced around Vega, letting loose quick jabs. Vega stood in the centre of the ring, turning to follow the dancing, circling Leonard. When the bell sounded to end the round, Dundee told Ray to sharpen up, slide inside, use some combinations, go in for the attack. In the middle of the second round Ray obliged. He quit dancing and went after Vega, banging away at his opponent with furious left-right combinations and racking up points on the three judges' scorecards. In the fourth round he let loose a string of vicious punches to Vega's face, causing his nose to bleed and gashing the corner of his left eye. The pace slowed in the fifth round, as both fighters took a rest, but in the sixth round Ray went again on the attack, forcing Vega into a defensive position. Dundee had told him to try to put Vega down, and obligingly Ray moved the Bull all over the ring.

When the final bell sounded, there was no question that the fight was Sugar Ray's, but Vega was still standing, his reputation for never having been knocked off his feet intact. He had indeed been a worthy opponent, and Ray couldn't help thinking that the fight had been almost like a replay of *Rocky*. Sugar Ray was the winner by unanimous vote of the three judges. His professional career had been launched in the best possible way, for he had fought well in a well-fought fight, proving that he was more than just a flashy amateur, and he had won. Moreover, with the money he had earned from that one fight he would be able to pay off his twenty-four creditors, at 8 per cent interest, and be beholden to no one. As he put it after the fight, he was a free man.

In April, Sugar Ray won his second pro bout, also by decision in Baltimore, this time against Willie Rodriguez. The large audience that watched the match at the Civic Center and on television attracted ABC-TV, which contracted with Ray to broadcast his fights on its 'Wide World of Sports', guaranteeing him not just money but a national audience.

His third fight, on 10 June 1977, took place in Hartford, Connecticut, and was staged by an unknown promoter named Dan Doyle, head coach of the basketball team at Trinity College in Hartford. The choice of unlikely venues was deliberate, as was the selection of little-known or unknown promoters. The Sugar Ray Leonard organization wanted to be a maverick in boxing – a free agency. Not only did Trainer and the others feel that they could make as much money as they needed by going that route, they also thereby avoided the complicated deals that marked the usual boxing promotions, which they felt they were not yet capable of controlling. Still, Doyle was an unlikely choice; he got into fight promotion in the course of writing a graduate-school paper on the subject. Doyle guaranteed Sugar Ray $12,000, and Ray earned that and more when he beat Vinnie De Barros by technical knockout.

Doyle later staged Leonard fights in Springfield, Massachusetts, and Portland, Maine, bouts that drew record crowds. The fight in Portland attracted more people than the Muhammad Ali – Sonny Liston heavyweight title fight in Lewiston, Maine, in 1965. Everything was going according to plan, and Trainer knew that if Sugar Ray could draw record crowds in small cities, bigger cities would become interested in staging Leonard fights.

Things were also going according to Angelo Dundee's plan to groom Sugar Ray Leonard for the big time. He continued to select opponents who could not beat Ray, but who were strong and varied in their boxing styles. Each new opponent was just a little bit tougher, forcing Sugar Ray to stretch his skills and develop new tactics each time he entered the ring. While this was a cautious way to develop a fighter, in Dundee's opinion it was the best way, and it was paying off.

As 1977 wore on, Ray piled up more, and more impressive victories, knocking out Frank Santore in five rounds in September, Augustine Estrada in six rounds in November, and Hector Diaz in a mere two rounds in December. By February 1978 when he had been boxing professionally just a year, he was meeting opponents for longer scheduled fights – eight rounds against Rocky Ramon in Baltimore on 4 February, a fight he won by decision. He KO'd Art McKnight in seven rounds in Dayton, Ohio. He was developing as a fighter so quickly that Dundee began to feel that the one-step-at-a-time method was too slow and insufficiently challenging for Ray.

For Ray's next opponent, Dundee chose Javier Muniz, who had stayed on his feet throughout a ten-round bout against Roberto Duran, a Panamanian known as one of the toughest and hardest-punching welterweights around. Muniz was an opponent with staying power in long fights, and Dundee wanted Sugar Ray to have the experience of boxing against him. But when Ray met Muniz in New Haven on 3 March 1978, it took him exactly two minutes and 45 seconds to knock him out.

Ray was the only one who was not surprised at the quick knockout. He had studied films of Muniz's earlier bouts and identified his weaknesses, and in the ring he went to work on them. He did not approach the fight game as a test of strength but as a test of talent, relying on cleverness, not brawn. He was as much a student of boxing as a practitioner, and he liked nothing better than to spend an evening with his videotape machine and a pile of cassettes of different fights. His approach to his career mirrored that of Trainer and Dundee: through a well-thought-out plan, they were slowly and deliberately working to making him the welterweight champion, and he was doing everything he needed to do to make that plan work.

Fighters can often be difficult for their managers and trainers to handle, slacking off on their training, overeating between fights, partying too much, overspending and getting into financial trouble, and forcing their trainers to act as babysitters. Sugar Ray, by contrast, was his own stern authority figure. He stayed in shape between fights, mostly by running, and made sure he got his rest. He did not party too much, allowed himself to gain only a few pounds over the 147-pound welterweight limit between bouts, and followed the advice of his financial advisers and trainers. It had been his decision to turn professional, and he did not expect anyone else to be responsible for him.

The structure of his organization and his financial arrangements with Trainer, Dundee and the others, also contributed to the general professionalism that pervaded Sugar Ray Leonard, Inc. There was none of the love-hate relationship that obtained between many other boxers and their handlers. Since Ray was not 'owned' by another man, he had no reason to resent his advisers, or to test the limits of their commitment to him in order to ascertain whether they were with him because they liked him or because he represented money to them. But Sugar Ray's professionalism also stemmed from his own single-minded determination to reach whatever goal he set for himself.

On he strove towards the goal of the welterweight championship, winning fight after fight against well-chosen opponents. Some people in boxing called them 'cream puffs', and remained sceptical of Sugar Ray's abilities as a fighter. At the same time, they were forced to admire Dundee's careful grooming of the young fighter, and the way Ray's organization managed to get his fights televised and bring in good money. It was a question of money, in fact, that caused ABC-TV not to renew its contract with Sugar Ray Leonard, Inc. – the network felt that Trainer was asking for too much. Ray's next two wins, a third-round KO of Bobby Haymon in Landover, Maryland, and an eighth-round knockout of Bobby Milton in Utica, New York, were not televised, but CBS broadcast the next, and Home Box Office, the cable TV channel, the following two. Sugar Ray Leonard was still the newest, most inexperienced, and lightest-weight fighter to be getting that much television exposure (heavyweight matches still commanded the most attention).

By the middle of 1978, Ray had advanced to ten-round bouts, winning by decision in ten against Rafael Rodriguez in Baltimore in June and Dick Ecklund in Boston in July, and knocking out Floyd Mayweather in the tenth in Providence. In October he won a decision against Randy Shields, who had beaten him in the AAU finals in 1974. In November he won another decision against Bernardo Prada in Portland, Maine, and he finished the year by knocking out Armando Muniz in Springfield, Massachusetts.

By March 1979, when he had been fighting professionally just slightly over two years, Sugar Ray began fighting world-ranked boxers, although that distinction was not as awe-inspiring as it sounds. Daniel Gonzales of Argentina was ranked Number 4 in the world, but

Muhammad Ali revitalized the public's interest in boxing.

After the big win against Vega.

Childhood sweethearts, married in Landover, Maryland.

Angelo Dundee checks Leonard's weight.

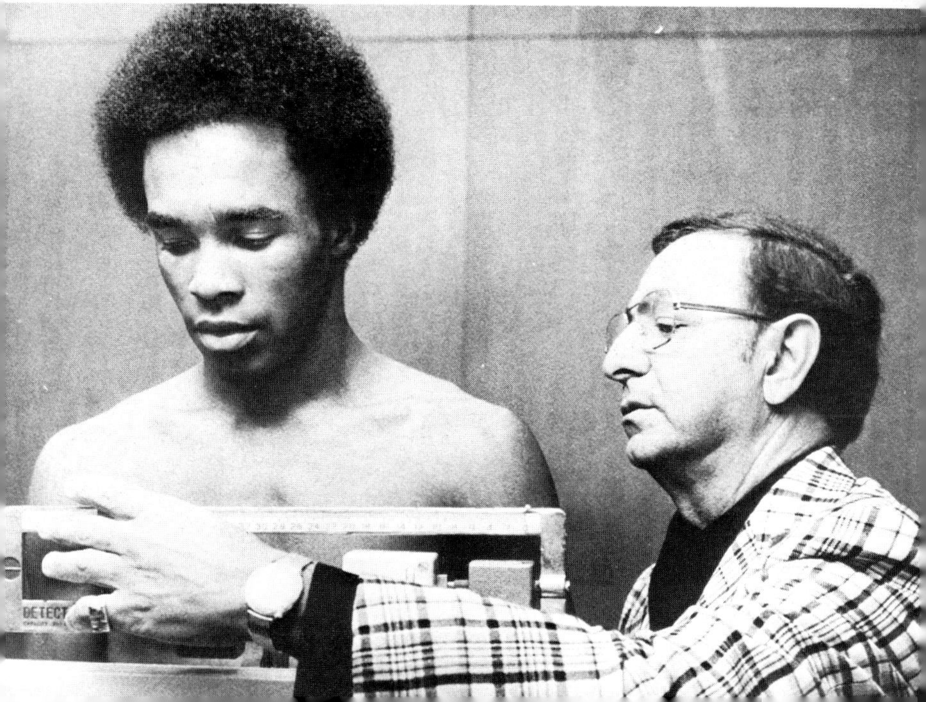

Duran won this one.

most of his victories had been against unknown fighters in Latin-American villages. Still, the fact that Gonzales held world ranking was helpful in promoting the fight on 24 March in Tucson, Arizona. And the prospect of fights against world-ranked boxers caused ABC-TV to come around with a hefty offer for television rights. ABC would chronicle the remainder of Ray's drive to the welterweight championship.

Sugar Ray prepared for the fight as usual, by training strenuously but also devoting a great deal of time to studying films of Gonzales' previous fights. As it turned out, he need not have bothered, for Gonzales' groupies did him in.

From the first, Ray had disdained groupies, partly because he had noticed how they seemed to drag down his idol, Muhammad Ali. By nature a loner anyway, Ray had chosen a few people whom he trusted, and discouraged hangers-on. Daniel Gonzales, by contrast, had allowed a great many people to attach themselves to him, and the effect too many such people can have on a fighter's performance was amply demonstrated that afternoon in Tucson.

Before the fight, in a room off a narrow corridor of the arena at Tucson Community Center, Sugar Ray Leonard warmed up under the watchful eyes of Janks Morton, Dave Jacobs and Angelo Dundee. Except for brief visits from his mother and Juanita, nobody was allowed near Sugar Ray. Ray had decided to try a new brand of gloves, which were more uniformly padded and made more impact than his old brand, which had more padding around the knuckles. After checking to make sure Ray's gloves were comfortable, Dundee sauntered out to the corridor and to the room next door, where Gonzales was.

The room was so full of people that Dundee couldn't see Gonzales. Men sat on chairs and tables, or leaned against the walls. Dundee's first thought was that with all these people in the room, Gonzales could not warm up properly, and when he finally spied Gonzales he knew he was right; the fighter wasn't even sweating. Dundee did not hang around but went back to Sugar Ray's room and told him to nail Gonzales at the first opportunity.

Ray knocked Gonzales down in the first round with a quick left-right combination. Although Gonzales got up immediately, he was none too steady, his eyes were glassy and he spat out his mouthpiece. Then Ray finished him off with a right-left-right combination, ending the fight after two minutes and three seconds. While some in the crowd cheered, others booed, feeling they had not got their money's worth. Even Getha Leonard was disgruntled: as was her habit, she had taken a tranquillizer before the fight, and she was hardly capable of celebrating her son's victory while tranquillized. Ray had exerted himself so little that he did not even need a shower.

His next fight, against Adolfo Viruet, was held in Las Vegas, a major venue for boxing matches, although the Dunes Hotel was not one of the more noted boxing sites on the strip. It had only a small arena, but Mike Trainer liked the idea of Ray's fighting in Vegas and knew the site carried more cachet than say, Tucson, Arizona, or Portland, Maine. This time the crowd, which numbered only about 2,000, got their money's worth, for the bout went the full ten rounds. Viruet represented a new challenge for Ray, for he was a left-handed fighter with an unorthodox style. In fact, some knowledgeable boxing men wondered if Dundee wasn't making a mistake. But Ray had adjusted to Viruet's style by the end of the second round, and in the fourth round he knocked down the Puerto Rican for the first time in his career. Viruet, furious at the insult, went after Leonard and was repeatedly warned for hitting low, elbowing and holding, but he failed to frighten Ray, to whom the judges awarded every round but the ninth.

For Ray's next fight, Angelo Dundee stepped up the pace of his training, and chose Marcos Gerldo. Once again, boxing insiders wondered if Dundee wasn't making a mistake, for in addition to being a tough hitter Geraldo was a 160-pound middleweight who had a good seven pounds on Ray at the pre-fight weigh-in on 20

March in Baton Rouge, Louisiana. But Dundee's purpose was to challenge Ray, and in the fight against Geraldo, Ray learned a lesson he would never forget.

In the third round, Geraldo landed a left hook solidly on Ray's head, the first solid punch to that area of his body that Ray had ever suffered. Dizzied, he tried to focus on his opponent, but could not; there were three Geraldos in the ring with him. Ray danced back and forth, trying to make the three images blend into one; he backed off, hoping that more distance would sharpen his vision. The three Geraldos came after him, and one of them hit him again. Amazingly, the second punch cleared his head, and the two shadow opponents merged into the middle one. But Ray was in trouble, for he'd been hit hard. To regain his strength and his timing, he needed more than a few brief moments in his corner between rounds; he needed to recover in the ring, and to turn the fight around.

He later said that he learned survival in that fight, that he had been forced to reach down deep within himself and to bring up every ounce of strength and will he had. He had to dance and feint as if his life depended on it, to buy time, to regain his rhythm. He succeeded, and won by decision the toughest fight he had ever fought. He also won new respect in boxing circles. More than a few observers had dismissed him as a phoney fighter created largely by the media and clever advisers, a fighter who'd had it too easy, who had never been tested, who'd been coddled and brought along inch by inch, who wouldn't show any stamina when the chips were down. Against Marcos Geraldo he showed that he had more than just speed and a bunch of pretty combinations; he showed that he also had strength and, most important of all, will.

The stage was now set for Sugar Ray to challenge Wilfredo Benitez, a Puerto Rican fighter and World Boxing Council welterweight champion. Ray's advisers contacted Benitez's manager, Jimmy Jacobs, who was eager to talk about a title fight against a young boxer with such media drawing power. Jacobs insisted that Benitez should get the larger share of the purse because he was the champion, while Trainer pointed out that Benitez had never earned more than $150,000 for a fight and that Sugar Ray was already earning more than that. Moreover, it was Leonard who would attract the audiences and the big money from television. In the end, they agreed on a 50-50 split.

Trainer then interviewed possible promoters and chose Bob Arum, who shared with Don King the distinction of being one of the biggest promoters in the game. Arum used his promoting expertise to ensure that the Benitez–Leonard fight would become one of the richest in the history of boxing, with each fighter guaranteed to make at least $1 million for his efforts, a first in welterweight history. The fight was set for 30 November 1979, in Las Vegas.

Meanwhile, Ray kept in shape by boxing Tony Chiavarini, a left-hander out of Kansas City, winning by TKO, and Pete Ranzany, the North American Boxing Federation welterweight champion, also winning by TKO. Sugar Ray Robinson attended this fight on 12 August in Las Vegas and made a point of telling reporters that he was honoured that Sugar Ray Leonard had adopted his nickname, a matter of resentment among some people in boxing circles who felt Ray Leonard had yet to earn the right to that respected moniker.

On 28 September 1979, Ray polished off Andy Price, a tough Californian who was supposed to have given him trouble, with eight seconds left in the first round; but this victory did not please Angelo Dundee, who'd planned the Price match as a warm-up for the Benitez fight, since Price's fighting style was similar to that of Benitez. Now, Ray would have to train very carefully if he expected to defeat the undefeated Benitez. Two long months stood between him and the most important fight of his life.

At twenty-one, Benitez was two years younger than Ray, but he had been fighting longer, having won his first world title at the age of seventeen and his second at eighteen. Currently, he was enjoying his second world championship, having won the junior welterweight title before claiming the welterweight crown. He was a clever fighter, with a varied style in which he was as good with his left hand as he was with his right. He was a counterpuncher, and some said he was the best defensive fighter in the game. He was also accustomed to going fifteen rounds, while for Sugar Ray Leonard this title challenge would be his first fifteen-round fight.

But Sugar Ray wasn't worried. In fact, a strange calm came over him as the big fight approached. As he put it, he started to feel 'settle-minded'. After two and a half years of intense concentration on each step to his goal, he began to think about his life as a whole, including his past and his future. Without losing sight of the Benitez bout, he was able to look beyond it. He realized he was nearing a major crossroads in his life, and that whatever road he took, that road had to lead somewhere. It would be time to pay some attention to his life outside the ring, and to get his life in order he knew the first priority was to marry Juanita and become a real father to Little Ray.

He shared his feelings with Nita not long before the fight, expecting that she would want to set the earliest wedding date possible. Juanita was overjoyed that the man she loved and the father of her child had finally decided to marry her, but she had her own ideas about how matters should proceed. She wanted a June wedding, she solemnly told her long-time fiancé; she had waited this long and she could wait until the proper month for a wedding. Laughing, Ray agreed. They announced the date just before Ray entered the ring at Caesar's Palace, Ray and his people ever mindful of a good human-interest angle on a fight. Win or lose, Sugar Ray Leonard would marry Juanita Wilkinson on 28 June 1980.

The night before, Muhammad Ali had called Ray with some well-meant advice about how to fight against Benitez, cautioning him not to try anything too cute or flashy. The judges would resent any hotdogging against a world champion, Ali said, and his advice made sense to Ray. He decided he would go toe-to-toe with the champion, and he began the fight in that stance. Leonard and Benitez stared at each other, their faces just inches apart, for a full thirty seconds at the beginning of Round 1, both aware that this was a big fight and both trying to gain an early psychological advantage. Sugar Ray made the first move. Jabbing with his left, working his left jab-right jab combination, he scored quickly against his opponent in the first round and again in the third round, when he knocked Benitez to the floor with a left jab. Through the third round, it looked as if Sugar Ray had the fight under control, but when the bell rang for the start of Round 4 the situation changed remarkably. A new Wilfredo Benitez seemed to come out of the opposite corner. Not only did he duck or evade most of Ray's punches, he started landing some of his own, scoring twice with his right in the fourth round while rendering Ray's right overhand practically useless with his defensive tactics. Angelo Dundee finally told Ray to forget that particular punch and 'go downstairs' to concentrate on body punches.

The fight was a rare display of ringcraft. Neither man was able to control the fight. Ray was amazed at how Benitez managed to evade his punches; no one had ever caused him to miss so many before. The part of him that was able to detach itself from the fight, that could figuratively stand back and watch what was going on, marvelled at how skilled his opponent was, and no doubt that same part of Benitez was thinking the same thing about Ray. Perhaps both fighters were too detached when they cracked foreheads in the sixth round and both went reeling back. Benitez got the worst of it. The collision resulted in a gash in his forehead, a wound that could be reopened with a well-placed punch from Leonard. Sugar Ray got only a welt on his forehead.

Benitez was hampered by the forehead wound and by a sore left thumb, which he had hurt earlier in the bout. He still cleverly defended against most of Ray's punches, but in the ninth round Ray scored with a combination that put Benitez up against the ropes. In the eleventh he delivered a hook with such force that it jarred loose his opponent's mouthpiece. But Benitez got in some scoring punches, too, and as the bell ended the fourteenth round neither fighter, nor the men in their corners, could be at all certain how the three judges had scored the fight thus far. Both believed they needed to win the fifteenth round, and they came out with a flurry of punches, trying everything they knew, reaching into their punching repertoires to come up with something that would catch the other off guard. Ray decided to try a punch he had been studying – a left uppercut that bantamweight Wilfredo Gomez used to great advantage. He'd been watching films of Gomez for weeks, and since his overhead right hadn't worked he decided to surprise Benitez with a punch that was almost the exact opposite. He stepped inside and delivered it, and Benitez went down on his knees. Though he was back up quickly, he was clearly dazed, and Ray took the opportunity to land two more quick punches. Referee Carlos Padilla stopped the fight with six seconds remaining.

It took Sugar Ray Leonard a few moments to clear his head before it dawned on him that he was the welterweight champion of the world. He had reached the milestone that he and Jacobs and Morton and Trainer and Dundee had been aiming for since he had decided to turn pro. He was the champ, and he had just finished the longest and best-fought bout of his young career. It was a proud night for Sugar Ray, and a proud night for boxing, because the two men had displayed the sport at its best and afterwards they had displayed sportsmanship at its best. At the post-fight press conference, even Benitez seemed exhilarated. Although the $1.2 million he would collect no doubt contributed to his attitude, he appeared genuinely pleased for the man who had just taken away his title. Sugar Ray was a great fighter, he told the assembled reporters. Wilfredo Benitez was a great fighter, Sugar Ray insisted. The two men embraced several times.

As it turned out, Sugar Ray would have won the bout by decision even without the TKO ruling by the referee, although by only two points out of a possible 136. Even if the opponents had been tied on the three judges' scorecards up to the moment when Ray had driven Benitez to his knees in the fifteenth round, there were few who criticized Padilla's decision to end the fight when he did. For as Leonard and Benitez went at each other in Las Vegas a middleweight boxer named Willie Classen lay unconscious in a New York City hospital, suffering from a brutal beating in the ring. He died a few days later, and the realization that boxing was at base a blood sport was very much on the minds of everyone in the fight game at that time.

Although his life had never been in danger during the title match, Ray was feeling the brutality of the game himself. He did not attend any of the post-fight celebrations of his victory. He had sweated so much that his body was dehydrated, every bone in his body ached, and worst of all, in his opinion, his face was bruised. In addition to the welt on his forehead he had bruises under his eyes, and he hated to have marks on his face. Still, in a way he felt as if the bruises were badges of courage.

At the age of twenty-three, Sugar Ray Leonard was welterweight champion of the world, at least of the world according to the WBC, for the WBA recognized its own champions. His possibilities for future matches were almost limitless, for not only did he hold the title, he was also credited with elevating the welterweight class almost single-handed to an importance approaching the heavyweight class of boxing. No other welterweight had ever attracted such large live audiences, or so much attention from television, or so much money for fights. He was now in a position to choose his opponents, to have the major say in where and when he fought, and to command ever larger purses.

He was also in a position to retire. He had done what he had set out to do, which was to become the champion and make a lot of money. Juanita reminded him of that, as did his mother. His advisers also remembered what he had said about wanting to stay in professional boxing only until he reached certain stated goals, goals which he had reached, and they were prepared to help him end his career in a dignified way. But Ray, having arrived at the point where he could retire if he wanted to, decided not to retire after all. He enjoyed being the champion, and he wanted to defend his title to show the boxing world that winning it had not been a fluke, that he was not just the WBC champion but the best welterweight in the world. And he still had the desire, voiced when he turned pro, to do something really big, something special.

Some people in boxing resented the fact that Sugar Ray was WBC welterweight champion, feeling that he hadn't paid his dues. He hadn't been in the game long enough or fought against opponents who were tough enough. He'd been coddled by his advisers, given too much money and too much media exposure in exchange for too little work. He was not in the traditional mould of the club fighter who slowly fought his way up through the ranks with little publicity and little money. He'd had it too easy, he wasn't a real fighter. Sugar Ray knew that much of this resentment stemmed from jealousy, but he still didn't like it, and it gave him the excuse he needed not to quit boxing. His new goal was to defend his title successfully, to prove that his victory was no flash in the pan. Besides, he would be a fool not to make a few more millions while he had the chance. He told Trainer to start considering requests from prospective challengers, and he told Juanita and the rest of his family that he was not ready to retire.

By this time, everyone close to Ray had benefited so much from his pro fighting career that they found it hard to argue with him. Just as he had set out to do, he had become the major, it not the sole, provider for both his families. He had been generous with his fight earnings; his parents had a new home in a nice section of Palmer Park and a hefty bank account; his father no longer had to work at the local supermarket and was Ray's official training-camp cook. His brothers and sisters had new cars and money for college, if they chose to go. But money had not turned the heads of his family. If Ray bought his parents airline tickets for a holiday, they were likely to turn them in and drive rather than fly in order to save money. Nor did Juanita change. She and Ray now had their own apartment, and Little Ray had all the clothes he needed, all the toys he could possibly play with. But as Juanita pointed out when people asked, she wasn't the one who was rich,

Ray was, he was the one who put his life on the line.

The people who had stood by him since the early days had not been forgotten. Dave Jacobs, for example, had a new house, two cars, and his own sizeable bank account; and Janks Morton had long before kissed the insurance business goodbye. Mike Trainer had drastically cut down his client list, for even on an hourly fee basis, he was making far more money working for Sugar Ray Leonard, Inc., than he could otherwise. And Angelo Dundee, even with only a 15 per cent share of Ray's earnings, was doing better than he had with any other fighter except for Muhammad Ali, although his financial relationship with Sugar Ray Leonard, Inc., would soon change. None of these people felt so beholden to Ray that they couldn't be objective about his decision, but all of them owed him enough to allow him to make his own choice.

Juanita's chief reaction to Ray's decision was to insist that they get married right away. Perhaps she feared that if he could change his mind about pursuing his pro career he could also change it about getting married. Juanita also wanted the world to know that the champion of the world loved her enough to marry her. She did not like the limelight, did not go around wearing lots of expensive jewellery or furs just because Ray was making big money, and refused to have a housekeeper or full-time babysitter for Little Ray, although Ray could afford it. But she did want to be married, not only in the eyes of the law but also in the eyes of other women. She tried not to feel insecure, but it had been hard, as Ray had become richer and more famous, to see how aggressive other women were towards him and to worry that he might decide to respond to their advances. She had deliberately refrained from making friends with women of her own age for fear that they might use her to get to Ray, but she realized that it would be even harder to control whom he met now that he was champion. She had always dreamed of a June wedding, but Juanita Wilkinson was accustomed to thinking realistically, and her intuition told her not to delay the marriage any longer.

Ray and Nita were married on 19 January 1980. Six-year-old Ray, Jr, was the ring bearer. They took a brief holiday in California and Las Vegas, and planned a real honeymoon trip for when Ray had more time. But even during this brief vacation, Ray couldn't get away from his boxing business. One day he picked up a newspaper and learned that there was a power struggle going on at Sugar Ray Leonard, Inc.

The source of the problem may have been Dave Jacobs, who had seen his influence on Ray and his career wane and was resentful of the power enjoyed by Trainer and Dundee, whom he considered newcomers to Ray's life, as well as the influence of Morton. Jacobs had kept quiet while Ray worked slowly and steadily towards the welterweight championship, but after Ray had beaten Wilfredo Benitez and claimed the WBC title, he had spoken up. He had not demanded more influence, because he knew that was futile, but he had demanded more money, telling Mike Trainer that he wanted a contract specifying 10 per cent of Ray's fight earnings.

When Ray returned from his holiday, he met Jacobs privately. Later, the announcement came that henceforth, Ray, Trainer and Morton would be the decision-makers, although both Jacobs and Dundee would be retained in essentially the same capacities as before. No one, however, would be paid a percentage of Ray's fight earnings: everyone would work for him on a fee basis, and this included Angelo Dundee. Dundee's contract had expired and Trainer negotiated a new contract with him under which he would be paid a fee, not a percentage. Many in boxing felt that the move was an insult to Dundee, but Dundee accepted the new arrangement and has never made a public statement about it. Had he been deeply insulted, he no doubt would have left Sugar Ray's employ. As for Jacobs, he stayed on but continued to resent both Trainer's influence over Ray and his comparative lack of it.

As champion, Ray was expected to defend his title at least three times in 1980. Already his first bout had been scheduled for 31 March, two months away. Juanita reminded him that when he did have time for a honeymoon she wanted him to be in one piece. To her mind, the odds were against his staying that way if he spent much longer in the ring.

Ironically, it was not Sugar Ray but the first challenger who really risked damage in the next fight. Britain's Davey (Boy) Green, a native of Chatteris, Cambridgeshire, had a record of 33-2, but many of his victories had been against boxing has-beens. His only previous fight outside his own country had been against a Danish fighter, Jorgen Hansen. He was ranked Number 10 by *Ring* magazine, and few boxing insiders believed he would be any real competition for Sugar Ray. In fact, the odds against him in the forthcoming bout with Leonard were six to one.

The choice of Green had more to do with money than with boxing skill, for there were other challengers, among them Pipino Cuevas, holder of the WBA welterweight title, a fight against whom would have been more interesting. But Bob Arum had been given an option on Ray's first title defence, and all he could offer Ray was $1.4 million, and Ray wasn't about to put his life and career on the line for that sum. The choice of a site for the fight was a political one. Originally it had been Las Vegas, but when it turned out that Ray's fight would be on the undercard of a Larry Holmes–Leroy Jones heavyweight title fight, both Arum and Trainer refused to take a back seat to Holmes. Instead, they chose Landover, Maryland, and billed the fight as a homecoming for Sugar Ray Leonard, the new welterweight champion.

From the opening bell, it was clear that Green was out of his league. Ray easily connected with flashy combinations. The second and third rounds were more of the same, with Green seeming to walk willingly into Ray's fists, getting off a wild swing on occasion. In the corner after Round 3, Dundee advised Ray to wait for an opening and knock his opponent out, and a little over two minutes later Ray obliged with a powerful left hook that he would later call 'the hardest punch I have ever thrown'. It slammed Green down on the canvas, and he did not move for several minutes.

They were the longest minutes Ray had ever suffered through, and he was forced to confront the wrong side of the boxing coin. The right side is boxing at its best, an intricate, even beautiful game when two opponents confront each other in a test not just of technique but also of will, when defence is as important as offence, when no one gets seriously hurt because both opponents are clever enough to evade savage blows. The wrong side of the coin is boxing at its worst, a brutal game in which improperly matched players are deliberately set up; or in which the players are well-matched but one gets caught off guard and is defenceless and the referee does nothing to stop the fight, or the attacker forgets that it is a game and moves in for the kill, or the attacker realizes exactly what has happened and gets the sinking feeling that in the course of the game he has done something that may mean the end of his opponent's career, or even his life.

Everyone who knows boxing knows that serious injuries, even death, can result when two men enter a ring intent on knocking each other out. Most of the time a boxer worries about getting hurt himself, but there are occasions when he is reminded that he is just as capable of doing harm. The two hands he has trained to put points on judges' scorecards are also capable of inflicting permanent damage on human beings. Boxing is neither game nor sport when one boxer permanently injures or kills another. When Davey Green fell to the canvas and did not move, Ray felt a cold, creeping fear spread over his entire body, numbing it, chilling his brain except for one terrible thought: what if he doesn't get up? And when at last Green did stir and finally got up, making it to his corner where a stretcher was waiting, the cold numb feeling did not leave Ray. He went through the motions of raising his arms and acknowledging his victory, but his mind was still on the question: what if?

For days afterwards he couldn't get out of his mind the image of Green lying motionless on the floor of the ring. He, who was so worried about even getting his face bruised, had delivered a punch so hard that it had knocked a man unconscious for several minutes. What would have happened if Green had been killed or suffered some permanent injury? Would the money and the media exposure, would anything, have been worth that human price? Did he really want to go on in this game that could be so brutal? A wiser Ray decided to continue his career with the personal knowledge that he wasn't just putting his own life on the line when he entered the ring. He was facing an opponent whose life he might also control.

5

Sugar Ray Meets Roberto Duran

BY THE TIME Ray had beaten Davey (Boy) Green, a lot of boxing people were saying that he was overdue for a real challenger. Many urged that his next fight should be against Pipino Cuevas, a Mexican fighter who was welterweight champion of the WBA, and whom many felt Ray had avoided for Wilfredo Benitez because he knew Benitez would be easier to beat.

Cuevas was a good opponent for Leonard, not just because of his prowess as a boxer but because a match between the two would unify the WBC and WBA welterweight titles. But for every fan of a Leonard–Cuevas match, there was at least one who wanted Ray to meet Roberto Duran, and many of the latter happened to be powerful in the WBA.

Duran was a Panamanian fighter who had made his career, his fame, and whatever money had come his way as a lightweight. He had only recently moved up to the welterweight class. Although Duran was a hero in his native Panama and enjoyed considerable celebrity elsewhere in Latin America, he had not made much money in his seventy-odd pro fights. Now, he and his managers were looking for a big fight, one that would get him the money and attention they thought he deserved. In their eyes, Sugar Ray Leonard was the key to it all. In the welterweight class, only a fight with Leonard could bring big television contracts and all the other perquisites that Duran had never enjoyed. But if Leonard fought Cuevas and lost, Duran would never get that chance.

A great deal of pressure was put on Cuevas to dissuade him from fighting Leonard. The WBA informed him that he could not meet Leonard in a title bout, to which Cuevas' people replied, that was all right, they would go for a non-title bout. But that wouldn't do either. Even if he fought Leonard in a non-title match, Cuevas was told, he would be stripped of his WBA title. In April, plans for a Leonard–Cuevas bout were cancelled without much explanation.

The World Boxing Association is based in Panama, and Panamanians have a great deal of influence on the organization. The president of the WBA, Rodrigo Sanchez, was a Panamanian by birth, and he was strongly influenced by the Panamanian government. This government wanted its native hero, Roberto Duran, to fight Sugar Ray Leonard, and put pressure on Sanchez to make the fight possible by influencing Cuevas not to fight Leonard to make way for a Leonard–Duran bout. One of Duran's people later insisted that the government had only 'requested' a postponement of the Leonard–Cuevas fight, but no one in the boxing world thought much of that weak explanation. Still, there wasn't much anyone could do but grumble about a conspiracy. The WBA and the WBC set their own rules, and they are both based in countries where the idea of government regulation has a different meaning from that in the United States.

Most boxing fans did not care what had brought about the Leonard–Duran match, but they looked forward to it with great excitement, for it would be a clash between fighters, and fighting styles, that were poles apart. Next to the prospect of such a match, considerations like unifying the welterweight title took a back seat. Who cared about the on-paper world champion? A Leonard–Duran fight would be a real contest.

Soon, promoters Bob Arum and Don King, who represented Duran, were talking terms, and their styles were as different as those of the fighters they represented. Arum, a lawyer like Trainer, looked as if he went to Wall Street every day. He wore pin-striped suits, visited a barbershop regularly, and approached fight promotion like an accountant, rarely letting his own personality get in the way of business.

By contrast, Don King's personality was part of his business, and he approached his business more like a circus ringmaster. Although he, too, dressed in suits, his hair stood out from his head as if he'd just put his finger in an electrical socket. This hair had become a trademark of sorts, and probably he needed a special hairdresser to keep it that way. A more conventional trademark was a crown, which was prominent at all the fights he promoted. There were always advertising poles in the ring with crowns on them, and often a huge crown emblazoned on the centre of the canvas. Don King, like most of the fighters he represented, had received his education in the streets. Like some of the fighters he represented, he had served a prison term for manslaughter. But he was no less smart than Arum, and he never let his own flamboyance get in the way of his money sense. Anyone who dismissed him as all flash and no sense wound up with a lousy deal or no deal at all. Arum and King squared off and before long they had a deal that would break all previous records for boxing revenues – a total projected to be as high as $30 million. The fight was set for 20 June 1980, in Montreal.

The only thing that the two fighters had in common was that both were excellent welterweights who had grown up poor, although by Duran's standards of poverty, Sugar Ray had enjoyed a privileged childhood. Born in Chorillo, a poor section of Panama City, Duran did not meet his father until he was twenty-one years old. The elder Duran was in the army and travelled around a lot, and each time he came home for a visit he left his wife pregnant but with no financial support. Roberto, the second oldest of nine children, could remember ten separate times when his mother had been forced to give him away to anyone who would feed him. There was never a time when he was not grubbing for food, spearing fish, stealing fruit, and fighting for scraps in garbage heaps. When he wasn't fighting hunger, he was fighting other kids, and he was expelled from school so often for fighting that when he finally dropped out at age fourteen he was only in the third grade.

Roberto started out in amateur boxing at the age of ten and fought exactly 16 amateur bouts (winning 13 of them) before he turned professional in 1967 at the age of seventeen. The purse for his first pro fight was $25.00. By the time anyone cared enough to train and guide him, his boxing style was firmly set; he was a street fighter and nothing could change his basic brawling, mauling style. What those who did train him managed to teach him was to be more scientific about his offence, and how to escape being punched back.

The young man whom friends called Cholo (rough translation: one whose hair is hard to comb) was a lightweight for most of his career, but if his weight was light, his punches were not. He bulldozed over opponents, winning by knockouts in the majority of his fights. It wasn't long before he received the professional nickname 'Manos de Piedra' (Hands of Stone). He did not lose a single fight during his first four years as a professional, then, at the age of twenty-one, he was beaten in a ten-round fight by Esteban DeJesus. He was furious over the loss, pounding the walls of his bathroom until his fists were bloodied and vowing to get even with DeJesus. He got the chance to do so twice, in 1974 and in 1978, and both times he won with savage knockouts.

By the time Duran met DeJesus for the second time, he was having trouble keeping his weight at the 135-pound limit, for he loved to eat and like many people who had grown up hungry found it nearly impossible to control his urge for food. He would balloon up to 170 pounds when he wasn't training for a fight, and even when he was in training his managers would almost literally starve him to ensure that he made weight. They knew that he would always get friends to sneak him a few steaks. By 1978 it was just too hard for him to qualify as a lightweight. After defeating DeJesus for the second time, he gave up his lightweight title and joined the welterweight class, the weight limit for which was 147 pounds.

He was equally successful as a welterweight, beating all eight of the opponents he faced. By the time his fight against Sugar Ray was set, he had won 69 professional fights, 55 of them by knockouts, and lost only once. Still, his punches had not been as devastating against the heavier fighters, and he had not been matched against more than a couple of fighters with prowess equivalent to his own.

Ray knew that Duran was going to be his toughest opponent yet. He knew about Duran's career and was aware of the excitement the impending match had caused in boxing circles even before the fight was officially announced. One sports writer called it the most anticipated non-heavyweight fight since Sugar Ray Robinson fought Randy Turpin and Carmen Basilio in the 1950s. Much of the excitement was blood-lust, in the expectation that if anyone was going to give Sugar Ray Leonard his comeuppance it would be the slugger and mauler Duran. Ray knew this, and found it hard not to be intimidated, especially after the press conference at which the fight was officially announced.

Some pre-fight showboating is *de rigueur* in boxing; it is expected that the fighters will pretend that they are out for blood, that they will try to gain an early psychological advantage by intimidating their opponents, preferably in clever ways that the sports writers can report in their columns the next day. Muhammad Ali was a master at it. Colourful reportage by sports writers would in turn generate interest in the fight, stimulate ticket sales, and attract TV advertisers. Ray knew this was an important part of the fight game, but that night when he faced Roberto Duran at the Waldorf-Astoria Hotel in Manhattan, he knew that Duran wasn't just playing. As the two men faced each other in front of the TV news cameras, Duran held his fist up in Leonard's face. 'June twentieth,' he said, 'June twentieth,' and his eyes told Ray what he planned to do on that date two months away. This wasn't just for the benefit of reporters and cameras; there was real hatred in Duran's eyes, and Ray was momentarily taken aback by the savagery of the man, even though he knew that Duran had once knocked out an opponent and then decked the man's wife as she stormed hysterically into the ring. Ray recovered quickly: 'When I fight Roberto Duran,' he announced, 'I don't just want to beat him. I want to kill him!' His eyes flashed, and he had a look on his face that those close to him had never seen before, at least not outside the ring. Later, when reporters asked him why he had not been his usual happy and glib self, he explained that he was just talking language that Duran would understand, and beating him to the punch. In Ray's opinion, Roberto would have said that he was going to kill him, if Ray hadn't said it first. Ray also assured reporters that he would not change his style to fight Duran, that he intended to beat him to the punch in the ring, too.

Sugar Ray was not interested in seriously injuring Duran, nor did he want to be hurt himself. He didn't want scars, or knots from calcium buildup, and he did not consider wounds a necessary part of fighting. All he wanted to do was stay in boxing long enough to defend his title successfully and make enough money to take good care of his family. He had regarded the fight against Duran as a business venture in which both would make a lot of money and he would be established as a top contender. But Duran had turned the coming bout into something more personal, and that both scared and excited Ray.

Both fighters went immediately into training. Duran and his entourage set up camp at Grossinger's, a resort in New York's Catskill Mountains. He trained harder than he had in years, aware that some people were whispering that he did not have the self-discipline to keep his weight down and get his body into top form. He knew that some people thought his age would work against him, for at twenty-nine he was five years older than Ray. He was shorter than the 5 ft 9 in Leonard by two and a half inches, his reach was seven inches shorter, and he knew that people were taking such statistics into account when they favoured Leonard to win. But Duran was studying films of Ray's fights, and though he regarded Leonard as a good boxer he was confident that he would emerge the victor.

Ray went to his training camp in New Carrolton, Maryland, where he, too, worked out with special determination. He studied films of Duran's fights, trying to find weaknesses and ways that he could use his own best moves to advantage. It was clear from the films that Duran usually controlled a fight, for he was good at cutting off the ring, forcing his opponents to stand still and fight. Once he'd cornered his opponent he had an essentially non-moving target for his hammer-like blows.

Although odds-makers favoured Leonard to win the fight by a 9 to 5 edge, there were many who questioned his ability to withstand Duran's vicious punches, and Leonard knew this. He felt a compulsion to stand up and 'fight like a man', and for this reason, plus what he saw in Duran's fight films, he disagreed with Angelo Dundee about the best approach to take against the Panamanian. Dundee wanted him to dance around, to feint left, to move right, to avoid getting caught on the ropes, to give himself room to make his left jab count. But Ray was determined not to run, and he was determined to put as much pressure on Duran as Duran put on him.

As 20 June approached, odds-makers continued to favour Sugar Ray, but even he admitted that Duran was winning what sports writers called the 'Psych Fight'. While Duran appeared confident, even cocky, in public, Ray became more withdrawn and nervous as the fight date neared. In Montreal, Ray Arcel, Duran's trainer, went about securing another advantage, or minimizing a potential disadvantage, lobbying against undue interference by the fight referee.

Refereeing a boxing match, like judging one, contains a heavy dose of the 'human element'. Some referees are 'active', calling many fouls and frequently breaking up clinches. Others are inclined to let the boxers go at each other and to step into the fight only when the most blatant fouls are committed. Because of Duran's fighting style, his people decided the latter type of referee was preferable, and in the final days before the fight they took steps to ensure that the referee, Carlos Padilla, would not be too active by publicly expressing concern that he would inhibit Duran and not allow him to fight his way, that he would call too many fouls and break Duran's rhythm. Later,

Angelo Dundee would bring the charge that by expressing those concerns Duran's people had inhibited Padilla.

Dundee should know. He had learned many tricks of the game from the wily old Arcel. Back in the 1940s when Dundee was just starting out in the fight business, he saw a fighter of Arcel's knock his opponent down. As the referee started to count, Arcel climbed into the ring and acted as if to throw a robe over his own fighter's shoulders. This action distracted the referee and confused him long enough to cause him to count the opponent out even though the man had actually got to his feet in time. Dundee thought this was a clever trick and later used it himself. Unfortunately, he couldn't figure out how to counter Arcel's intimidation of Padilla.

The final days ticked away, and suddenly there was a new problem. In the course of a pre-fight physical that included an electrocardiogram, Duran showed signs of a heart condition. He submitted to further tests, and the official verdict was that his heart had given off so-called abnormal patterns because he was a particularly powerful athlete who happened to have a cold.

To help promote interest in the fight, there was an official weigh-in on Wednesday, 18 June, two days before the bout. Leonard and Duran sat on opposite sides of the room, and Duran kept holding up two fingers and shouting, 'Two more days. Two more days and I am champion.' In response, Ray smiled and blew a kiss at Duran, calling back, 'I love you,' in a vain attempt to throw the guy off-guard. Duran's response was a string of Spanish epithets. Sugar Ray admitted that he was a little afraid of Duran. The Panamanian's style, reactions, character were like nothing he had ever encountered before. Ray told reporters. 'He's so – what do you call it – ferocious . . .'

On the night of 20 June Montreal's Olympic Stadium was packed with over 45,000 people, ranging from the beautiful and the famous in $500 ringside seats to the average folks who'd paid $20 to sit under the rafters. There was a buzz of anticipation throughout the preliminary fights, which this night included a bout in which

Ray's brother, Roger, who had turned pro after getting out of the Air Force, beat Clyde Gray in a junior middleweight contest. When it was over, Roger triumphantly returned to the dressing-room he shared with Ray, and was puzzled when his younger brother congratulated him in a distracted way. Roger asked what was wrong, but Ray wouldn't confide that he felt lost. Suddenly, all the momentum and excitement had vanished. He had got caught up in the publicity, in the verbal sparring with Duran, all the stories about Duran's savagery and bad-guy image, all the questions about whether he could take Duran's punches. He had thought he understood the media and how to use them for his own benefit. He had believed that he could play the media game without losing his concentration or taking personally what went on. But he had underestimated the power of Duran and of the media hype, which he later compared to a spider's web and himself to a fly.

Duran entered the ring first, blowing kisses to the crowd and raising his arms to his cheering supporters. Then Sugar Ray arrived. As he entered the ring, he thought about how he had fought in the same arena back in 1976. After the Olympics he had wanted to quit boxing. Now here he was back again, hoping that a win tonight would make it easier for him to retire soon. But, as he later said, there was no adrenalin flowing through his body. He went through the motions of waving at his cheering supporters, but he felt like a robot. Instead of playing to the crowd, as he could do so well, he simply opened his arms as if to accept the homage due him. Then he turned to Duran for the traditional pre-fight tap of gloves, but Duran refused the tap, scoring another round in the 'Psych Fight'. As if to add insult to injury, both Duran and his wife gave Juanita the finger, which shocked Juanita and Sugar Ray.

The three judges from three different countries signalled that they were ready, the referee gave his instructions, the opening bell rang, and the two fighters squared off, jockeying for position. Ray dealt out a lightning-quick left jab that found its target, but that was the one good punch he managed in the entire three minutes. Duran just swarmed over him, driving him towards the ropes with a furious flurry of punches. Always moving forwards, he forced Ray along the ropes from one corner to another, scoring repeatedly with lefts and rights inside. To Ray and his supporters, the three-minute round was like a nightmare in slow motion.

In the second round, Duran again took immediate control, forcing Ray to the ropes. He caught him with a solid left hook followed by an overhand right and pinned him in the corner for most of the round. Referee Carlos Padilla did little to control the infighting, and when the gong sounded Sugar Ray looked dazed.

By the end of the third round, Juanita was crying in her ringside seat, and Ray's younger sister, Sharon, was trying to comfort her. To most people in the arena it looked as if the scheduled fifteen rounds could go no more than five rounds. Ray just wouldn't be able to hold up under Duran's mauling. But Ray showed that he was made of stronger stuff. The punch in the second round might have dazed him, but it also woke him up to the realization that he had to start fighting back. By the fourth round he was standing head to head with Duran, clutching, grabbing, fighting it out. Even the men in Duran's corner were awed by his courage and amazed at some of the punches he took. For a full two rounds the boxers were like the proverbial immovable object and irresistible force.

By the sixth round, Ray was managing to break away from Duran's clutches once in a while, and when he did he made good use of his opportunities, scoring with jabs and left-right combinations. He continued to hold his own through the seventh, eighth and ninth rounds, but it took every ounce of strength and concentration he could summon up. He didn't even notice when Juanita fainted in the eighth round.

As the fight continued, Sugar Ray tried but failed to get control; it was pretty much Duran's match the whole way as they stood slugging at one another. But Ray never gave up, and Duran never brought him to his knees. The thirteenth round was the finest of the match. It was extraordinary that either fighter had the strength to get through it, let alone put on such a superb display of ring skill. As usual, Duran quickly got Ray into a corner of the ring with a left hook, but Ray just as quickly slipped away. Duran found his mark with another left hook and then dealt Leonard a right. Ray delivered a right of his own with such force that Duran's head snapped to the side. Then they clutched each other and traded body blows. Ray's combination of three lefts to the body and two rights to the head were a major factor in his being awarded the round by two of the three judges.

The Panamanian let up in the last two rounds, but not because he was too tired to keep up the pace. Instead, he was still psyching out Sugar Ray Leonard. In the last round, as he jabbed with his left he tapped his own chin with his right. Then he simply walked away, making street-gesture references to Leonard's manhood. Refusing to let Duran think he was intimidated, when the final gong sounded Sugar Ray raised his arms in a victory sign, telling the crowd he believed he had won the fight. Duran rushed up behind him and knocked his hands down. Ray approached Duran for the usual glove tap at the end of a bout when no one has been knocked out, but Duran refused the gesture.

Although he had put on a confident front, Ray was almost certain that Duran had won, and was not surprised to learn that the decision in Duran's favour was unanimous. The French judge had awarded six rounds to Duran, four to Leonard, with five too close to call. The English judge had awarded six rounds to Duran, five to Leonard, with four undecided. Only the Italian judge believed that the fighters had been so evenly matched that a full ten rounds were too close to call. Of the other five rounds, he had awarded three to Duran and two to Leonard.

Roberto Duran was the new WBC welterweight champion and the third man in boxing history to have won the championship in both the lightweight and welterweight classes. He had made a lot of money from this fight, but perhaps most important to him, the whole world had seen him win, for the fight had been carried on closed-circuit television in many places and would be broadcast on commercial television in a variety of other areas. For a man who had grown up as poor as Duran, who had been forced to fight for food and for sheer survival, this was a sweet victory. He even forgot his animosity towards the man he had beaten. In the pandemonium of his locker room after the fight, asked by reporters how he felt about Sugar Ray Leonard, he yelled, 'Leonard, you're my friend now,' but by then Ray was in his own locker room, out of sight and out of earshot.

If Roberto Duran's victory was sweet, Sugar Ray's loss was bittersweet. In many ways he had done what he set out to do, to show the world that he could indeed take a punch, that he wasn't just a dancer and prancer without the courage to put his pretty-boy face on the line. He could not imagine anyone questioning his courage now, for he had met the toughest opponent possible and shown just as much skill and talent as he had displayed in earlier fights against lesser opponents. Duran might have controlled the fight, but he had never overpowered Sugar Ray. The judges might have awarded the decision unanimously to Duran, but not one of the three had awarded Duran more than two rounds over what they had scored for Leonard. People were calling the fight a magnificent, memorable combat, and that was something of which Ray could justifiably be proud. Moreover, the money he had earned for the fight was more than five times what Duran would realize, and Ray was in the business of boxing for the money.

But even a man who approaches the fight game in such a businesslike manner cannot help being affected by losing, particularly for the first time in his professional career and especially to a man like Duran. The Panamanian might be a superb fighter, and Ray was not taking anything away from him for that, but he was the exact opposite of so much that Ray believed he stood for. In Ray's eyes, Duran symbolized the side of boxing he didn't like, and the fact that raw fury, unsportsmanlike behaviour and macho viciousness had beaten him did not sit at all well with Sugar Ray Leonard.

'What are you going to do now, Ray?' the reporters wanted to know, even before he'd had a chance to shower and have his bruises attended to. Even if he had felt like answering, Ray could not have responded because he did not know. Most of his plans had depended on a win in Montreal. He was at that moment supposed to have been the champion of the world, and from that lofty perch he would have decided whether it was worthwhile to remain in boxing. But he wasn't champion of anything now. He had lots of money but no title, and his natural pride made him averse to the idea of retiring a loser.

On the other hand, the bruises on his face and the stiffness in his muscles reminded him that continuing in boxing would mean more of the same, and he also had an aversion to that. He'd received remarkably few injuries in his career and was not accustomed to seeing physical proof that he had been through a bout. After the Benitez fight, he had been upset over the discoloration under his eyes and a lump on his forehead, and those bruises were nothing compared to what he saw in the mirror now. His whole face was puffy and sore. He had knots on the back of his head, and his left ear was swollen and twisted from Duran's repeated right hooks and from the rubbing of Duran's head against his during their many clinches. Studying his ear in the mirror, all Ray could think about were the cauliflower ears he'd seen on so many old fighters. That night, so sore that he could barely move, he decided he was a fool to take such abuse any more. 'This is it,' he told Juanita, and she breathed a sigh of relief.

Juanita had gone to pieces watching Ray take that kind of punishment from Duran. To her mind, the money wasn't worth the risk of injury, and she didn't want Ray to take any further risks. She was not alone in feeling this way. Mike Trainer, who had nurtured Ray's career for four years and enjoyed the experience immensely, had not enjoyed seeing Ray in the ring with Duran. Trainer had from the beginning put Ray's interests ahead of his own, holding no 'piece' of Ray, and so he hadn't that much to lose except his hourly fee if Ray quit boxing. As far as Trainer was concerned, Ray could retire immediately if he wanted to. Dave Jacobs, Janks Morton and Angelo Dundee concurred. In fact, there was no one close to Sugar Ray Leonard who had any desire to try to persuade him to go on with his fighting career. It was all up to him.

6

Sugar Ray's Revenge

NOT LONG AFTER the Duran fight, Ray and his wife and son took their long-awaited honeymoon, a ten-day holiday in Hawaii where they swam and sunbathed and walked along the beaches. Gradually, the swollen places on Ray's face and the knots on the back of his head, the infection in his ear, and the soreness in his body went away. But the internal wounds remained, and his mortification at having lost to a man like Roberto Duran festered. He constantly replayed the fight in his mind, regretting that he had done this or not done that, and getting away from the mainland United States did nothing to quell the memories. Everywhere he went in Hawaii, people recognized him and encouraged him to stay in boxing: 'You'll get him next time, Champ,' they said. Ray sensed pity in their voices, and hated its sound. He did not want to be pitied for losing to a man like Duran.

Pride may well have caused him to lose the fight. The night after the bout, Juanita had asked him why he had just stood there in the early rounds and let Duran maul him. Ray had answered that he'd wanted to prove he could take a punch, that he didn't want people saying that Duran could have knocked him out if he hadn't spent the whole night running away. It was not necessary for Juanita to remind him that he'd proved he could take a punch, but had lost the fight. They talked about his retiring from the ring, agreeing that they had enough money to live comfortably for the rest of their lives. The bruises on his face and the knots on the back of his head had bothered them both, as had the memory of the strain on Juanita as she watched her husband take Duran's punishment. That need never happen again, he need never climb into another ring. But they agreed, too, that retiring as a loser might be harder to deal with than any of the physical or psychological pain. Ray's own image of himself was as a winner, and he had to make that image real again.

First, he had to accept the fact that he had lost, and that took time. A month after the fight, he was insisting that his title had been 'confiscated', that he had watched films of the fight and in his opinion he had scored more points than Duran. Duran had bulled him and pushed him up against the ropes, but he had connected with more punches and his punches had been cleaner. He was not alone in feeling that way. Some sports writers agreed with him, and it was their columns that he read and re-read during the weeks after the fight.

But most sports writers and boxing experts thought otherwise, including 'trainer extraordinaire', Angelo Dundee. Although Dundee thought the officiating had been lousy, he also believed that Ray had allowed Duran to control the fight, fighting Duran's fight instead of his own. Dundee had warned him against this during training, but Ray had refused to listen to him. Dundee didn't say, 'I told you so' to his young fighter, but he did want Ray to accept the loss and take responsibility for it. Whether he quit or stayed in boxing was not as important as dealing realistically with the loss. If he was going to continue to feel robbed, he would never have the confidence either to put boxing behind him or to win another fight.

While still in Hawaii, Ray made his decision to continue in boxing, and specifically to fight Roberto Duran again, and win. Once again he had a goal, and in fact this was his most important goal to date. This rematch with Roberto Duran would be for his manhood. He told Trainer and Dundee to contact Duran's people about a rematch, but they were not interested in such a bout in the near future. Nor was Duran. Thanks to the media exposure he'd received for the fight against Ray, the Panamanian was now a bankable commodity. Why risk another fight against Leonard? A rematch too soon would not generate enough public enthusiasm, and so it would not generate enough money. Moreover, WBC rules forbade immediate rematches, and although such rules could always be waived, it was not customary to have immediate rematches in boxing for a number of reasons.

Other fighters had to be given a chance at the title. If a boxer had lost a title, or lost in a title match, he should not get an instant rematch. There were also the important considerations of public enthusiasm; too frequent title matches would pall on the public as quickly as would a second baseball World Series featuring the same teams six months after the first. Muhammad Ali's three fights with Joe Frazier had been spaced over five years – in 1971, 1974 and 1975 – twenty months had separated the last two.

With no prospect of an immediate rematch with Duran, Ray did have an alternative: he could try for a fight with the champion of the WBA welterweight division. Pipino Cuevas and Thomas Hearns were set to vie for that title in the autumn, and Ray could try for a fight with the winner of that match. But Ray wasn't interested in any fight but a Duran fight, and he asked his people to keep up the pressure for the only fight he wanted. He sensed that Duran would consent to a rematch if he were offered enough money, and he suspected that if both he and Duran wanted the fight the WBC would find a way to bend its rules.

Trainer, Morton and Dundee were willing to do as Ray wanted. Only Dave Jacobs disagreed. He was not convinced that Ray could beat Duran in an immediate rematch, and he feared that a second loss would mean the certain end of Ray's career. He was for bouts with other boxers to give Ray more experience; there ought to be at least one warm-up fight before he met Duran again. But Jacobs was overruled, and he decided that was one time too many. Saying he could not stay on and help Sugar Ray work for something he did not himself believe in, Jacobs quit the Leonard organization.

Jacobs had not been happy with his role for a long time. He had been with Ray from the start; his wife had cooked dinners to finance trips to amateur boxing competitions. He'd trained Ray at the Palmer Park Recreation Center when the 'ring' was four strips of tape on the basketball court. He had driven Ray's family and friends to Montreal in a sardine-can van to see Ray win the Olympic gold medal. When Ray had turned pro, he had stayed on in the role of trainer without a contract, because he had an understanding with his young friend. He had profited from their continued relationship, but he had also seen his own influence slip, especially after Ray won the WBC welterweight championship and Jacobs had been publicly humiliated by the announcement that henceforth Trainer and Jacobs would be making the major decisions with Ray. He had stayed on, but he did not get along with Mike Trainer, and he had often thought of leaving. But he still had a great regard for Ray, still felt like a father to him, and could not pull away. He stayed on through the Davey (Boy) Green fight and then through the Duran fight, but after his advice about how Ray should proceed was not taken, he felt he had to leave.

The departure of Jacobs left a crack in the image of Sugar Ray Leonard's 'second family', which his fight-business associates had often been called. It bothered Ray that money and power considerations had created this crack, but he was realistic enough to understand that it was a rare 'family', business or otherwise, that did not suffer from the pressures of success. In some ways he was relieved not to feel pulled in opposite directions by advisers with differing ideas, for Morton and Trainer had often disagreed with Jacobs. With Jacobs gone, Janks Morton now had sole responsibility for Ray's day-to-day training.

Meanwhile, Trainer and others worked at getting a rematch with Duran. Before long, Carlos Eleta, Duran's manager, had agreed to it, persuaded by the promise of big money. The $1.5 million Duran had earned from the first fight was going quickly. His wife, Felicidad, had decided to open a clothes boutique in Panama, and that would take an investment of several hundred thousand dollars. And Roberto's expenditures were considerable, for he had many friends and hangers-on.

Another important reason why Eleta wanted the fight

was to force Duran back into training, for he had put on weight very quickly after the Leonard fight and Eleta didn't want him to get too heavy to qualify as a welterweight. It was possible that he could lose the title without ever having defended it. So, Eleta told Don King to negotiate terms with Mike Trainer, and in September he ordered a 173-pound Roberto Duran back into training.

Don King was in a position to call the shots this time, and he drove a hard bargain. In the first fight, Duran had netted $1.5 million to Ray's $9 million. This time, the figures would be $8 million for Duran and $6 million for Leonard, not an inconsiderable sum for Ray, who was a proven audience-draw, win or lose. The official announcement came on 2 October and the title rematch was set for the New Orleans Superdome on Tuesday, 25 November 1980. WBC president Jose Sulaiman was on hand to explain that the organization's rule against immediate title rematches had been waived 'for the good of boxing'.

The good of boxing notwithstanding, there was much bad will surrounding the match, and it was not the kind that made for good publicity. If the two fighters were brought together, no one could be sure that they wouldn't start the match right then and there. So they were kept apart as much as possible, and when they did meet, breaths were held on both sides. Right after they signed for the rematch, Leonard and Duran filmed a commercial for Seven-Up in New York with their two sons. Don King had a talk with Duran and urged him not to taunt Leonard on this occasion. Everything went smoothly at the filming, possibly because of the presence of the two young boys, but perhaps also because neither man wanted to risk losing the money promised if the commercial filming went well.

Ray had been in training since he had made his decision to fight Duran again, but now he began intensive training, which oddly enough, now that Morton had sole responsibility for the day-to-day training of Sugar Ray, involved *less* work. In the past, in Morton's opinion, Ray had worked too long and too hard to prepare for a fight. This time he was to keep in shape only by running. They went to Ray's training camp in New Carrolton, Maryland, a week later than usual, and even there Ray did not train as hard as was customary. While in the past he had sparred as many as fifteen rounds a day, every day, now he sparred no more than nine rounds a day, and every so often Morton told him to take a day off. But in terms of strategy, this was the most intensive pre-fight training ever.

Ray sparred against heavier opponents, who were instructed to fight in Duran's style, crowding and mauling him, cutting off the ring and pinning him against the ropes. In response, Ray had to work on developing his hand and foot speed inside, in tight situations, and he worked hard to shorten his left hook. Angelo Dundee arrived the first week of November, earlier than usual, to help out with classroom sessions in which they viewed films of the 20 June fight and Dundee pointed out that Duran was not the stupid bull of his reputation. On the contrary, he had a very clever technique, for as the films showed he was constantly doing things to keep Ray off balance, switching his feet, waving his hands, feinting, grabbing Ray's head, shoulders, elbows to upset Ray's rhythm. According to Dundee, the only way to deal with these tactics was to counter them with similar moves. Never just stay in front of him, Dundee warned, never spread your feet so wide that you cannot move quickly, never back up in a straight line, and do not lie against the ropes. Move from side to side, switch your feet, feint, too, and as soon as you feel the ropes on your back spin out. As the night of the fight neared, Dundee would actually get into the ring with Ray and his sparring partner and go through the various positions of arms, feet and head, step by step.

Sugar Ray Leonard was training to fight smart. He was going to show Duran and everyone else that the championship belonged to him. He was going to win so decisively that no one would ever question his abilities again. And this time, *he* was going to psych out Duran, make him look bad, make him look crazy. But he was going to do this in the ring, not before the fight. Everyone agreed that another pre-fight 'Psych War' would not be good for Ray, and the Leonard camp was uncharacteristically closed-mouthed as the fight approached.

When the two fighters arrived in New Orleans (Duran from a training camp in Miami, Florida, because the weather was too cold for him in the Catskills), Angelo Dundee broke the silence of the Leonard team. A week before the scheduled bout, he publicly expressed his concerns about two things: the first was the length of Duran's beard, which Dundee charged he had used as a weapon in the previous fight, scratching Leonard's face. Dundee wanted Duran's beard trimmed, but officials of the WBC and the Louisiana State Athletic Commission did not think that was called for.

Second, remembering how Duran's people had intimidated the referee the last time, Dundee asked the Louisiana State Athletic Commission to spell out its definition of fouls such as butting, holding and grabbing, explaining that he wanted to make sure its definitions accorded with his. Duran, Dundee charged, also used the top of his head as a weapon, so much so that he should be required to put a glove on it. Duran had committed the fouls of holding and grabbing repeatedly when he had Leonard against the ropes in the last fight. By charging that most of Duran's fouls in the fight had not been called by the referee, Dundee hoped to ensure that the referee on 25 November would be an 'active' one.

Sports writers were relieved when Dundee spoke out, for there had been so little said by either side thus far that it was hard to file stories about the fight. The only angle on the fight was the lack of public excitement it inspired. Ticket sales were lagging, although part of the reason was no doubt the fact that seats were twice as costly as they had been for the previous fight. Another reason was scheduling. Sure, people wanted to see Duran and Leonard fight again, but it takes time to fan public excitement to fever pitch.

Ray did not much care about the lagging ticket sales. By agreement, he would be fighting for a guaranteed sum, not a percentage. Mike Trainer had insisted on that, not wanting his business-minded fighter to feel that he had to promote the bout to assure himself a nice profit. But Ray, for the first time in his pro career, was not in a fight for the money. He would have fought for a dollar if necessary.

His pride was at stake in this fight, as was his career. He knew he would not be able to go on in boxing if he lost to Duran a second time. What he would do and how he would feel about himself for the rest of his life depended on this fight, and for this reason he was again favoured to win, although not by as many points. While in the first fight the odds had been 9-5 in his favour, now they were 3-2. In addition to factors like the age difference of five years and Ray's being in better training shape, both of which made it easier for him to bounce back quickly from the gruelling fifteen-rounder on 20 June, odds-makers had rightly taken into account the factor of motivation, which in an individual game like boxing is more crucial than in a team sport, and there was no question but that Ray had strong motivation to win. He had not been able to forget Duran's obscene gestures, the way he had tapped his own jaw with one glove while hitting Ray with the other, the way he had refused the traditional glove taps. Every time Ray thought of Duran's unsportsmanlike behaviour he seethed inside. But this time he refused to allow emotion to overpower him; instead he used it to increase his motivation. Sugar Ray was out for sweet revenge.

It was expected that the two men would appear together at a pre-fight press conference, and they obliged, although Duran kept his hands tucked under his arms the whole time, possibly to avoid making involuntary obscene gestures. Even the official weigh-ins on the morning of the fight took place separately. Both men weighed exactly 146 pounds. Duran had clearly been forced to struggle to make weight. He'd been at 160 as recently as the first week in November and at 148 earlier that very day. Right after the weigh-in he gulped down a Thermosful of beef broth and ate two oranges, an indication that he was dehydrated, having dieted so strenuously that his body was suffering from a lack of moisture. His beard was measured and deemed a suitable length. Ray was pleased with his weight, for the last time he had weighed 144 and had dropped to 140 in the course of the contest. With added weight, he felt he had added strength.

There was an odd occurrence at the weigh-in. Although

Ray arrived at the Superdome first, it was boxing protocol that the champion be the first on the scale. So, Ray went straight into the room where Dr A.J. Italiano of the Louisiana State Athletic Commission was waiting to examine both fighters. Meanwhile, Duran arrived and was weighed, but instead of changing places with Ray and going next to Dr Italiano, he was swept out of the weigh-in room and towards the Superdome exit by his large group of followers, none of whom seemed to understand English and thus the instructions to proceed next to the doctor. Fortunately, Duran's interpreters arrived and he was taken to the doctor's office. Some people in Ray's camp charged that the delay had been deliberate, that Duran's blood pressure or heart-beat were too high. But Dr Italiano pronounced him ready to fight.

Thomas Hearns had beaten Pipino Cuevas for the WBA welterweight title some months earlier, and seemed to regard the Leonard–Duran rematch as a personal insult. He had fully expected that he would be Ray's next opponent, that he would win the fight and then beat Duran for the WBC title. When the Leonard–Duran match was announced, he had charged that Ray did not have the guts to fight him and Duran did not have the talent. He had bad-mouthed both fighters, and at the rematch, at every opportunity, and on the day of the fight he succeeded in getting a few more headlines by sending each a live turkey.

On the night of 25 November, 35,000 people entered the New Orleans Superdome, failing to fill even half the 79,758-seat capacity of the arena for what had been billed as the 'Fight of the Century'. But the atmosphere was lively as the crowd sat through the two preliminary fights. Roger Leonard and Mark Holmes, brother of WBC heavyweight champion Larry Holmes, both took their matches. As ten o'clock neared, the crowd buzzed with expectation, and when Sugar Ray Leonard entered the hall they cheered delightedly.

There had been no sudden loss of will or concentration for Ray this time; he was 'up' and felt good, and he was ready. He came down the aisle preceded by cheerleaders waving pom-poms and chanting 'Sugar Ray, Sugar Ray!' and his enthusiastic supporters joined in the chant. Ray smiled happily and waved to the crowd, but his eyes were deadly serious. As if to underscore his determination to be tough this time, he had departed from his usual custom of wearing white and had dressed entirely in black: trunks, socks and boxing shoes. Before the fight, he had asked Mike Trainer how he looked and had been pleased with the response, 'like the Grim Reaper'.

Then the champion made his entrance to the blare of salsa music and the waving of hundreds of small Panamanian flags. The cheering was not as loud for Duran. Ray's namesake, Ray Charles, sang a rousing rendition of 'America the Beautiful', and Sugar Ray smiled as he listened to the song, looking relaxed and confident. Duran scowled, but he too looked confident.

When the opening bell sounded, Ray came out circling, moving in and out. Duran was also cautious for the first minute. Then he saw his chance and bulled Ray to the ropes, but Ray did not stand and fight. He quickly slipped away and landed the first punch of the bout, a grazing right. The two traded quick punches, then Ray landed a straight left and a hard right to the mouth. Duran smiled as the bell ended the round. As the second round began, Duran immediately forced Leonard to the ropes, but the Mexican referee, Octavio Meyran, separated them as they clinched. Ray faked away and laughed. The same scene was replayed twice more in the round. Ray was not letting Duran control the fight but instead was dancing, circling, shifting from side to side. Duran's timing seemed to be affected, for he missed several shots. Once again at the buzzer, Leonard landed two swift jabs.

Duran regained his timing in the third round and connected with several punches, managing to bull Ray to the ropes and keep him there, twice. But Ray fought well inside, and neither man was the clear winner of the round. In Round 5, Ray slipped to the canvas about the same time as Duran landed a right to his body, but the referee, Meyran, ruled it a slip, not a knockdown. The referee wiped the resin from the ring floor off Leonard's gloves. This round was too close to call.

In the sixth round, Duran seemed continually short on his jabs, as if his timing was off again. Leonard's, by contrast, were right on the mark, and he continued to control the fight, making Duran come after him and frustrating his opponent's bulling tactics with his constant dancing and circling. The ring floor was in bad shape by now, a floorboard in mid-ring having split. One section had sunk down several inches, and had probably caused Ray to slip. After the bell to end Round 6, both Ray Arcel and Angelo Dundee tested the sinking area and agreed that the fight should not be delayed because of it. In Round 7, as Ray and Duran fought, workmen attempted to repair the ring from underneath. Duran again regained his timing in that round, landing an early hook to the head and another to the stomach and pushing Ray to the ropes. Ray answered with a hard jab to the body. He had been dancing around throughout the fight. Now, he began to taunt Duran, dancing and circling and not throwing any punches. Duran scowled at the clowning. Leonard continued to dance and suddenly was aware that he had Duran watching his feet. 'I've got him now,' Ray said to himself. As if in confirmation, the voice of ringside commentator Howard Cosell came through to him: 'Duran is completely bewildered!'

Still taunting, Ray wound up his right arm as if to throw a bolo, then suddenly changed and came at Duran with a left that struck him square in the face and made his eyes water. There were hoots of laughter from the crowd. Ray opened his eyes wide in pretended fright and stood flat-footed, jutting his chin out, daring Duran to take his best shot. He went into the Ali Shuffle moving his shoulders from side to side, arms dangling at his sides. He faked a windup with his right arm and motioned for Duran to come to him. Sneering, Duran body-punched him into the ropes, where the two went at each other in a furious exchange of punches.

At the start of the eighth round the referee decided there was too much Vaseline on Duran's body and insisted on towelling some of it off. When the fight resumed, Leonard began moving from side to side, flicking jabs at Duran, and like a bull after a wily matador Duran charged at his opponent and tried to force him to the ropes. Leonard backed up and scored a hard right to the jaw, then landed two left jabs and a left-right-left combination that staggered Duran. With about a minute left in the round, Ray had Duran backed into the ropes when suddenly Duran dropped his hands to his sides and said, '*No mas*' – No more. It took the startled Sugar Ray only an instant to realize what that meant. Duran didn't want to fight any more. He, Sugar Ray, was the winner. He leapt into the air in triumph.

Referee Octavio Meyran would not hear of Duran's quitting. He signalled Leonard to continue fighting, and Sugar Ray obliged, turning and delivering a hard left-right combination to Duran's body. Duran didn't even try to defend himself. '*No mas,*' he said again, and this time the referee did not try to overrule him. At 2 minutes and 44 seconds into the eighth round of a scheduled fifteen-round fight, it was official: with a technical knockout Sugar Ray Leonard had regained the WBC welterweight title. Curiously, Duran, who had refused to touch gloves with Leonard in Montreal, now embraced the new champion before he left the ring – but not before Roger Leonard had leaped into the ring and thrown a punch at him.

At first a stunned silence fell over the crowd in the Superdome. Then there was an uneasy murmur as people turned to each other and asked, 'What happened?' As everyone recognized that the fight was over, the reactions were understandably varied. Some cheered Leonard, others booed Duran, and still others shouted 'Fix! Fix!' Never before, in all of boxing history, had a champion walked away from his title so unexpectedly and inexplicably. Never had there been a more bizarre ending to a title bout. And never in the world would anyone who knew boxing have believed that Roberto Duran, the veritable personification of the word *macho*, would just up and quit. Why, he'd sooner die in the ring – or so everyone had thought.

Muhammad Ali had once continued fighting with a broken jaw. Henry Armstrong had gulped down blood for five rounds before a referee had threatened to stop the fight if Armstrong kept bleeding. There was a time back in 1949 when middleweight champion Marcel Cerdan was forced to quit with a pulled muscle in his right shoulder and Jake LaMotta had been awarded the title, but Cerdan's had been a definite injury. Roberto Duran looked fine. In the confusion after the Superdome fight ended, there were rumours that Duran had cramps in his stomach, in his legs and arms, and that he had a separated shoulder. But the doctors who examined him after the fight could find absolutely nothing wrong with him.

So why had Duran quit? He had fought a good fight. At the end of the seventh round, two of the three judges had scored Leonard ahead four rounds to two, with one round tied, and the third judge had scored them even closer, four rounds to three. Duran could have pulled himself together – he had seven rounds in which to do that. There was speculation, fed by rumour, that he was hurt in some way. But there was also considerable speculation that what was injured in Roberto Duran was his pride. Leonard had taunted him, teased him, and caused him to lose face, and like the typical neighbourhood bully he could not take the insult. When he couldn't shut Leonard up with his fists, he didn't want to play any more.

In his locker room after the fight, Duran informed his associates and friends that he was retiring from boxing. Even those who yelled 'Quitter!' loudest couldn't help seeing the sad aspect of what had happened. Duran, who had won 72 out of 74 fights, including 41 straight victories, scored 55 knockouts, and had 13 successful title fights, would be remembered best for the one fight from which he had walked away.

Life was not going to be easy for Roberto Duran. He had a party in his locker room after the fight was over, but he realized that his name was going to be mud in his native country. He had planned to fly from New Orleans to New York with his wife and son. Orders to cancel those plans and return immediately to Panama soon came, direct from General Omar Torrijos, Panama's president. Being the number one national hero, Duran was also regarded as a national possession. It would be difficult for him in

Panama, a small country of about two million people, every one of whom knew who he was. There would be no place for him to hide.

In his own locker room, Sugar Ray Leonard avoided criticizing Duran. As champion, he could of course afford to by sympathetic, but there was more to his reticence than that. Ray understood that something had to be wrong with Duran, mentally or physically, to cause him to walk away from the fight. Despite his intense personal dislike of Duran, Ray had always respected him as a fighter. Also, Ray's idea of good sportsmanship meant not kicking a man when he was down. Angelo Dundee felt the same way. He objected to the word 'quitter' as applied to Duran. Try as they might, sports writers could get no words of rancour from the Leonard camp, not even from Roger Leonard, who had been so insulted as a boxer by Duran's action that he had jumped into the ring and punched him.

Still, there was a shadow over Ray's happiness at having regained the championship. He would have preferred a decisive win – a knockout, or at least a technical knockout after the full fifteen rounds. He knew he had proved he could control the fight and make Duran box his way and that he was the better fighter. But he did not like the idea of a victory surrounded by so much controversy. He was preoccupied after the fight, when ordinarily he would have been celebrating. He didn't even react when Thomas Hearns threw a rubber chicken at him. He didn't have time for Hearns' antics at that moment.

Later on, after the full impact of what had happened really sank in, Ray began to see the bizarre victory in a different light – as the sweetest kind of victory. He had *made* Duran quit. He had done exactly what he had set out to do – to make him mad, make him crazy. To force a man like Roberto Duran to give up was even better than knocking him out.

Ordinarily after a championship fight the winner gets more publicity than the loser, but the 25 November fight at the New Orleans Superdome had been no ordinary fight. If they were not bemoaning the state of boxing, sports writers were more likely to write about Roberto

Duran than Sugar Ray Leonard. Their concern about the state of boxing was justified. During 1980 there had been two major fights that had been downright embarrassing for the sport. Earlier that year, Muhammad Ali had come out of retirement yet again to meet heavyweight champion Larry Holmes in Las Vegas. The fight had been scheduled for fifteen rounds, and the thirty-eight-year-old Ali had stood up gamely for ten of them. But he had taken a terrible pounding and his people would not let him go out for the eleventh. Later, Ali admitted to having taken an overdose of weight-reducing drugs and to being weak and dehydrated as a result. People had paid high prices to see the fight live or on closed-circuit TV, and understandably they felt cheated. Then came the Leonard–Duran fight, and this time the fans didn't just feel cheated, they felt downright hoodwinked. Something had to be done to ensure that such things would not happen again, or so the sports writers claimed.

There was a brief attempt to withhold Duran's share of the fight purse, but there was no way to do that legally. Instead, Duran was fined $7,500 for not performing up to WBC standards. WBC officials decided to look into the matter of stiffer fines, but for the time being all anyone could do was hope that the two embarrassing fights in the same year were flukes. Two days after the Superdome bout, boxing was embarrassed even more when Roberto Duran declared that he had decided not to retire at all and wanted a rematch. He did not get his wish. In the eyes of most people in boxing, Duran had dashed his chances of ever again being taken seriously as a fighter.

The question that plagued sports writers and boxing fans was why had Duran quit, and there was much newspaper space devoted to possible reasons. But the answer could come only from Duran himself, and he was not talking. Although there was evidence that he might not have been completely well physically, that he might have had problems with his heart or blood pressure and that he most assuredly had been forced to diet much too strenuously to make weight, the general consensus of opinion remained that his real problem had been hurt pride. Sugar Ray Leonard, the man whom Duran had psyched out even before the Montreal fight began, had subjected him to the most sustained humiliation he had ever suffered, and he simply couldn't take that humiliation for another seven rounds. So, he had chosen to dismiss Leonard, saying in effect, 'If you won't come in and fight like a man . . .' But his strategy had backfired. The macho men saw no strength in that. They only saw a quitter.

7

Champion of the World

IT TOOK Sugar Ray Leonard some time to come down from the high of his victory over Roberto Duran, for he had concentrated so intensely on winning that post-fight life seemed meaningless by comparison. But that was often how he felt after an important fight. He knew that the feeling of emptiness would pass and that he would soon have another goal, another bout to train for. He knew he ought to make the most of the in-between time and enjoy a period when boxing was not the most important thing in his life.

He went on long walks with Juanita, who liked to tell him that such walks helped put things into perspective, that seeing the beauty of Nature made people's problems seem smaller, and their triumphs, too, for that matter. Walking in the park, Ray realized that beating Roberto Duran had not been such an earth-shaking event and that the world seemed to be going along much as before. He also spent time with Little Ray, mostly playing basketball, softball, football. He was reminded that he had never spent much 'quality time' with his son and hoped Little Ray did not hold that against him. He hoped to be a better father to the other children he wanted to have with Juanita, although he wasn't sure when that would be since she had told him she wanted to wait until he retired from the ring and had time and attention to devote to other children. There was little discussion of his retiring at this time. Even Little Ray wanted him to fight Thomas Hearns, and beat the man who had thrown a rubber chicken at his dad.

There would be no immediate bout with Hearns. Mike

Trainer had a plan, with which Ray agreed, that would take advantage of the opportunities Ray now had both to make a lot of money and to develop further as a fighter. The plan took into account the WBC rule that a champion must defend his title three times a year against one of the top ten contenders. For Ray, it also presented an opportunity for him to gain a special place in boxing history by adding to his welterweight title the junior middleweight title.

Step One called for Ray to meet Larry Bonds in Syracuse, New York, at the end of March. Bonds, a twenty-nine-year-old sanitation worker from Denver, was an unknown who had not even fought for a year, but then Trainer was not looking for a fight between Leonard and Bonds. As he put it, their meeting would be an 'event'. Trainer wanted to show that Sugar Ray Leonard could fight a virtual unknown in a small city and still draw a crowd. He claimed that people would pay to see Sugar Ray in any circumstances.

Syracuse was no stranger to prize-fighting. Years before, the city had hosted some major fights with such contenders as Carmen Basilio and the DeJohn brothers, but there hadn't been a title fight in Syracuse since Billy Backus had beaten Jose Napoles for the welterweight crown eleven years before. Not surprisingly, Syracuse rolled out the red carpet for Sugar Ray Leonard, and he responded with equal grace, making a number of publicity appearances and signing hundreds of autographs every day. Angelo Dundee announced that Sugar Ray would display in Syracuse a new punch, 'a Carmen Basilio uppercut, with either hand'. Finally, tickets for the bout were going to be priced with the 'little people' in mind. The top price would be $60, and only 15 per cent of the seats would be sold at that price. The remaining 85 per cent would be priced at $20 and $10. These prices were a far cry from the $1000 and $5000 ringside seat prices at Montreal and New Orleans. Obviously, Ray was not going to make much from live gate receipts, but Trainer expected to net him about three-quarters of a million dollars from cable-television broadcasts of the fight.

As expected, Leonard easily defeated Bonds in the ten-round bout which was viewed live by the 21,000 people who filled Syracuse's new, domed arena. Thousands more watched the fight on cable TV. Added to that, 6,000 spectators, many of them children, had attended Ray's six pre-fight workouts in Syracuse. Mike Trainer kept careful track of these attendance figures, for he intended to use them when negotiating terms for the really big fight that lay ahead – against Thomas Hearns, or the man whom Hearns had beaten for the WBA welterweight title, Pipino Cuevas. If Ray could draw as many spectators as that for a fight in Syracuse against a sanitation worker from Denver, just think of how many people would pay to see him compete against a world-ranking opponent.

Trainer and Dundee had had another reason for choosing Larry Bonds for the bout in Syracuse: he is a left-hander, and Ray had not fought a southpaw since beating Adolfo Viruet and Tony Chiaverini two years earlier. He needed practice against left-handers in the event he went up against Thomas Hearns.

Ayub Kalule, a right-hander who fights like a left-hander, was chosen as Ray's next opponent. Once again, it would not be a title defence. On the contrary, Ray would be the challenger in this bout, for Kalule was the WBA junior middleweight champion. Weight for boxers in that class is 154 pounds, and Ray would have no trouble making weight. In fact, it was clear that he would soon have to move out of the welterweight class, for at twenty-four he was still growing. He had grown a half inch taller in the past year, there was new muscle growth in his neck and thighs, and his muscularity was bound to increase even more. He would be a bona fide middleweight before long. In the meantime, he had the opportunity to experiment in the higher weight class, and just possibly he could hold two titles – welterweight and junior middleweight – simultaneously.

Twenty-six-year-old Ayub Kalule was a Ugandan of the Baganda people who lived in Denmark and who had been unbeaten in all of his previous thirty-six fights, half of them victories by knockout. Although he was not known in the United States, he was respected in international boxing circles as a fine man and a powerful, though not brilliant, fighter. No one expected him to beat Leonard, but he would be a worthy opponent. The match was scheduled for 25 June at the Houston Astrodome.

Meanwhile, Mike Trainer and Angelo Dundee had arranged for Ray to meet Thomas Hearns, in the fight that the boxing world was waiting for, on 16 September in Las Vegas. A Hearns fight 'on the same card' as Leonard–Kalule in June would promote the September bout. Thus, on 27 April, two days after Hearns successfully defended his WBA welterweight title against Randy Shields, it was announced that on 25 June Thomas Hearns would fight Dominican Pablo Benitez. During the negotiations between Leonard's and Hearns' representatives, Emanuel Steward, Hearns' manager and trainer, had at first wanted the Hearns–Baez fight to be last, at the prime time of 10 p.m., but he changed his mind when Trainer pointed out to him that the media would not give the last fight much coverage if they were all busy interviewing Sugar Ray Leonard.

Bob Arum volunteered to promote the Leonard–Kalule fight. One of his press agents, Irving Rudd, decided to garner publicity by capitalizing on Kalule's Ugandan background and bring in a witch doctor. Not knowing any witch doctors personally, Rudd called the Ugandan Mission to the United Nations in New York City and was referred to Ben Mugimba, a witch doctor who claimed he could make rain, stop a tornado, and put curses on people. He was also a Catholic with six children who had once operated a gas station in Kampala and was presently running a coffee plantation. Mugimba was flown to the United States to summon the support of the spirits for Kalule and to put a few curses on Sugar Ray Leonard.

Sugar Ray, whose ability to recognize a potential publicity-garnering promotional stunt was considerably greater than his sensitivity to the racist implications of the plan, thought it was funny and even decided to embroider it a bit. He sent someone to the library to research Ugandan witch doctors and, learning that they are supposed to fear the colour black and don't like snakes (too fast-moving to put a spell on), he ordered a special outfit for the fight. His black robe had yellow serpents on the sleeves and his black trunks a yellow cobra on the left leg.

When he was introduced to Mugimba at a press conference, Kalule was understandably offended. Charging that Rudd must think him a fool, he reminded everyone that he had not just come out of the jungle. Ray wore his anti-witch doctor outfit to the fight anyway.

In Houston, in a fight not worthy of prime time, Thomas Hearns took care of Pablo Baez in the fourth round of a scheduled ten-round bout. Then Sugar Ray and Ayub Kalule squared off for their fifteen-round fight. It was expected that Ray would dance around Kalule in the ring and force his opponent to come after him, but he surprised the crowd by going right after the Ugandan with lightning-quick jabs against which Kalule seemed unable to defend himself for two full rounds. Then, in the third round, Ray threw a left hook at Kalule's head and injured his own middle finger, an injury he had suffered several times before. The finger hurt every time he jabbed at his opponent's head but would not hinder a hook to the softer target of Kalule's body. Still, the injury clearly handicapped him, for his left jab was the trigger for all his combination punches. To compensate, Ray came out roaring in the fourth round with a flurry of punches that caused Kalule to lose his balance four times, though he did not fall. Kalule was known as an iron man, and he had never been knocked down.

In the next round Kalule began to find his rhythm, and midway in the seventh round he knocked Ray off balance with a right that actually spun him around. Suddenly, it looked as if the careful plan might crumble. What if Sugar Ray lost to Kalule? What if experimenting in a higher weight class turned out to be a mistake? As Kalule appeared to gain even more confidence in the eighth round, a foul-up in the careful plan seemed all too possible.

Then, in the ninth round, Kalule fell apart. With his left hand hampered by the injured middle finger, Ray unleashed everything he had with his right. Two hard punches to the head drove Ray to the corner, but he got off two solid rights before Kalule could get away. Then Ray went after Kalule, and with another right he put his opponent against the ropes. He then unleashed two savage left-right combinations, and Ayub Kalule, who had never been knocked down before, hit the canvas. The referee, Carlos Berrocal, began the count, but Kalule, though dazed, was on his feet at the count of six. Berrocal asked if he was all right and Kalule shook his head, no. The referee signalled that the fight was over. Ray had won with a technical knockout.

Ray had been practising a special acknowledgement of his win. He leapt into the air and did a no-hands flip that delighted the crowd. It was an entertaining finish to an interesting and well-fought bout, and a fitting reaction for a man who now held both the WBC welterweight and WBA junior middleweight titles.

The attention of the boxing world now shifted completely to the forthcoming Leonard–Hearns fight. The bouts in Houston had generated excitement primarily because people had a chance to make judgements about how Leonard and Hearns would do against each other. Now boxing fans, and the fighters themselves, seemed to be saying, 'Let's get this over with. On to the big one.' Representatives of both fighters had agreed by contract that the bout would be described only as a fifteen-round welterweight fight; no title was mentioned because both sides feared that one of the world boxing associations might object. Sugar Ray Leonard was in a unique position: he held the WBC welterweight championship, and there was no problem with that. But in beating Ayub Kalule and gaining the WBA junior middleweight title he had broken the WBC rule against holding two titles in different organizations at the same time. Everyone involved hoped to iron out the problem over the next couple of months, so the Leonard–Hearns fight could indeed be a bout to unify the welterweight title; but they thought it best not to make mention of titles in the contract for the fight.

That contract called for Ray to earn at least $8 million and Hearns $5 million, a lesser guarantee because although they were theoretically champions of equal stature Ray was clearly the bigger drawing card. The contract carried two stipulations concerning the way the fight would be advertised: 1) Half the advertisements for the bout would call it the Leonard–Hearns match, and the other half, the Hearns–Leonard match; and 2) When fight-night came, a coin would be flipped to decide who would enter the ring first.

Both fighters knew that if they could attract a large live audience and a huge cable-TV audience they stood to garner far more money than the guarantees stipulated by contract, and within two weeks of the 25 June bouts the hyping of the 16 September match had begun. The two boxers need hardly have bothered, for they were already recognized as the two most exciting fighters in their weight class, if not in the game of boxing as a whole, and the public had been anxious for a showdown for months. Even Ray stated publicly that this was one fight that needed no hype. But pre-fight hype functions not only to engender interest in a fight, it also serves the contenders as an outlet for their serious attempts to psych out their opponents long before they enter the ring.

Ray had no illusions about beating Hearns easily. The man's nickname was 'The Hitman', and the Detroiter was tough and clever. He also had important physical advantages: at 6 ft 1 in tall, Hearns had three inches in height over Leonard, and his reach was four inches longer. Moreover, he was three years younger. But Hearns, for his part, was taking Sugar Ray Leonard seriously, for in addition to his boxing skill he had more experience dealing with big-fight hoopla, having gone through it not once but twice, in connection with his bouts against Roberto Duran.

The two fighters actually liked each other personally. The live-turkey gifts to Leonard and Duran before the second match and the rubber chicken-throwing incident after that fight had not been Hearns' ideas, but those of a public relations man. Hearns had felt silly carrying out that plan. Although his public image was not apple-pie nice, as was Ray's, Thomas Hearns, too, was a likeable fellow, kind of shy, a family man. Born in Memphis, Tennessee, in 1959, he had grown up in Detroit. His father had left the family early, and Thomas and his seven brothers and sisters had been raised by their mother, poor but proud. Hearns had managed to escape the enticements of crime and drugs that were rampant in his neighbourhood by spending most of his out of school hours boxing at the Kronk Recreation Center. He had started boxing at the age of eleven when he was a scrawny 55 pounds, but with the help of Emanuel Steward, the Center's boxing trainer, he had worked his way up in the amateur ranks. He and the older Ray Leonard were not often on the same national teams, but they had met through amateur boxing. Hearns won both the Golden Gloves and national AAU titles in 1977 and turned pro the same year. Sitting at ringside and cheering him on for his first professional fight, which he won by a knockout, was Sugar Ray Leonard.

An integral part of a boxing match is the 'Psych War', but at first Hearns did not take part in it. He had nothing bad to say about Leonard, he said. He also warned, however, that he had a boiling point and that Ray should not allow him to reach it. For his part, Ray was generally gracious when he spoke to the press about Hearns, but because of his greater charisma and greater sense of ease with the press he scored points in the 'Psych War' from the start.

Construction began on the huge, 25,000-seat temporary boxing arena on a tennis court adjacent to Caesar's Palace in Las Vegas, and arrangements were made by the promoters of the fight for on-site ticket selling, 300 closed-circuit TV sites, and nearly twenty cities on pay television (the first time ever for a major sporting event). One of the lesser promoters, but still a long way from his term paper days, was Dan Doyle, who had promoted some of Ray's earliest pro fights. With his partner for the venture, Shelly Finkel, a rock music promoter, he had the New England closed-circuit TV rights. He had approached Mike Trainer about promoting a Leonard–Hearns bout by himself back in 1978, but Trainer had suggested that they should wait, and now Doyle was delighted that the deal had not gone through. Back then he had planned to offer Leonard $100,000 and Hearns $12,000, hoping to make a few thousand himself. Now, even with just half of the New England closed-circuit TV rights, he stood to make much more, for the fight promised to be one of the richest in history.

At this relatively early stage, people who really knew boxing were about evenly divided on who would win. Those who favoured Hearns pointed to his age, height and reach advantages, to his superb jab, and to how he had fought against Pipino Cuevas to capture the WBA welterweight title in the summer of 1980. Cuevas had never been beaten, never even been knocked off his feet or visibly hurt; yet Hearns had knocked him out cold midway in the second round.

Those who favoured Leonard cited his intelligence, his ability to learn with every new fight and to adjust to his opponents in mid-match. They also considered him to be a far more experienced fighter when it came to big tests, for Hearns had defended his title only three times since winning it from Cuevas, and none of his opponents had approached the power of someone like Roberto Duran. He had knocked out Luis Primera in six rounds, been awarded a technical KO against Randy Shields, and beaten Baez in Houston.

While others speculated on the outcome of the forthcoming match, the two fighters trained. As usual, Ray's sparring partners were chosen on the basis of how similar they were in physique and style to his future opponent, which in this case meant being taller, with a longer reach. Such requirements excluded Odell Leonard, who had been one of Ray's sparring partners on a fairly regular basis since 1974. Many people had assumed that Odell was Ray's cousin, but they were not related. Odell Leonard's real name was Odell Davis, and he had come under Dave Jacobs' wing in 1974; he was still under the management of Jacobs. After a fairly good amateur career he had turned pro, but he had made extra money as a sparring partner for Ray. He'd changed his last name to Leonard after Ray had won the 1976 Olympic gold medal, hoping to capitalize on the famous last name. Ray Leonard knew that he had changed his name and why, had been both flattered and annoyed, but had let it pass.

When Odell Leonard was turned down as as a sparring partner in Ray's training for the Hearns fight, he went to the Hearns camp and was hired. Some assistants to Emanuel Steward, Hearns' trainer, worried at first that Odell Leonard was a spy, but once they learned that the two were not related and that Odell had been rejected as a sparring partner for Ray, they realized he would be useful. Also hired as a sparring partner for Hearns was Lloyd Taylor, another fighter managed by Dave Jacobs. But the big news was that Dave Jacobs had himself joined Hearns' camp.

Dave Jacobs and Emanuel Steward had been friends since both had coached US amateur boxing teams. Jacobs had worked with Hearns as an amateur, just as Steward had worked with Leonard when he was an amateur. Aware that Jacobs had left the Leonard organization, Emanuel Steward had invited him to become a trainer for Thomas Hearns. When they heard the news, Sugar Ray and his people were furious. Janks Morton told the press that Ray had paid for Jacobs' house and two cars, besides putting a large sum in his bank account. What kind of thanks was it to join the camp of Ray's opponent? Ray himself did not comment publicly, but he was angry as well, and even after his anger subsided he was hurt by the action of the man to whom he had been so close for so long.

Jacobs bore no ill-will against Ray, and he had mixed feelings about taking the job. He wasn't quite sure what he was supposed to do as a member of the Hearns team. He knew that Emanuel Steward did not need any help training Hearns. He appreciated that he could be useful because he knew so much about Leonard, but he also realized that his main value would be psychological. Sugar

Ray Leonard might be able to psych out Thomas Hearns with words, but the presence of Jacobs in the opposing corner of the ring was obviously calculated to psych out Leonard.

By September, the Leonard–Hearns/Hearns–Leonard bout, called simply a welterweight match in their contract, was being touted as a fight to unify the welterweight title. The various problems with the WBA and WBC had been ironed out. Not since Roberto Duran had knocked out Esteban DeJesus on 21 January 1978, to consolidate the WBA and WBC lightweight titles, had there been a unification match. For various reasons, this consolidation of titles in September 1981 was not expected to last long, but it was one more reason for excitement over the bout. An even greater cause for excitement was how evenly matched the fighters were. When betting on the fight opened in Las Vegas, Leonard was an 8 to 5 favourite, but that was primarily because he was better known. As fight night approached, Hearns was favoured 7 to 5, but few betters made their wagers with certainty. Sports writers and sportscasters were compelled to choose one or the other fighter, but nearly all admitted that the bout could go either way.

Still, more experts picked Hearns and the reasons were boringly familiar to Ray: he'd had it too easy; he'd never really been hurt; he'd never been knocked down in a pro fight, and according to boxing wisdom until a fighter is knocked down even he does not know how he will react to the shock and embarrassment and whether he will be able to stay and fight; he had not proved that he had, as *New York Times* sports writer Dave Anderson put it, 'the soul of a gladiator'. (Anderson predicted that Hearns would knock out Leonard in the fifth round; most others who favoured Hearns thought the fight would go at least twelve rounds).

It was all very exasperating for Sugar Ray Leonard, who asked himself, 'What do I have to do to prove myself – get killed?' Had everyone forgotten the Benitez fight, the first Duran fight? He'd got hurt in those bouts. The querying of his toughness was getting dog-eared, but people kept at it. Weren't people ever going to take him seriously in spite of his 'pretty face' and all-American image? Psyched up, not psyched out, Ray determined to beat Thomas Hearns through artistry, to go inside and deprive his opponent of the advantage of that long reach, to get him confused, hit him in the body, and knock him flat.

On 16 September 1981, Hearns and Leonard had their last meeting before the crucial fight when they participated in the official, pre-fight weigh-in. Surprisingly, Hearns weighed in at 145 pounds, a pound less than Leonard. Ray studied his opponent and decided that whatever he had done it would eventually weaken him in a long fight.

On the night of 16 September, the night of the third 'Fight of the Century' in the last two years, every seat was filled at the temporary arena built on the tennis court of Caesar's Palace, and had been sold, for prices ranging from $50 to $500, within days of the stadium's completion. The seating arrangements in the arena were planned in a masterly way to force those who yearned for exposure the maximum amount of it for the maximum price. Only money talked, and so former heavyweight champion Sugar Ray Robinson was relegated to a $50 seat while little-known 'profilers' were in the $500 limelight. It was a star-studded crowd, comprising movie stars, hustlers, entertainers at the various casinos on the Strip, important people from the athletic world, and just about every top-ranked American boxer, as well as former champions like Muhammad Ali and Joe Frazer and the aforementioned Sugar Ray Robinson, all sweltering in the 100-degree heat of the early desert evening.

As provided for by contract, there had been a coin flip to decide who would enter the ring first. Sugar Ray had won and elected to enter last, taking for himself the advantage of the grand entrance. Hearns bounced into the ring, displaying the legend on the back of his robe – 'Winner Take All' – to the cheers and applause of his fans who remembered his pre-fight statements that he would take away Leonard's title *and* his Seven-Up commercial. At his request, Hearns was introduced as the 'Motor City Cobra', a reference to his hometown of Detroit, Michigan, the centre of the automobile manufacturing industry.

Sugar Ray then arrived to cheers and applause of equal volume. The back of his robe read 'Deliverance' – a reference to his being tired of having Hearns around as a challenger.

The three judges, all Las Vegas men, were introduced, and the referee, Davey Pearl, outlined the rules of the bout. If a fighter was knocked down, he had to take a mandatory eight count; a fighter could not be saved by the bell except in the fifteenth round; scoring would be on the ten-point system, with the winner of a round getting ten points and the loser anything below that. Sugar Ray Leonard and Thomas Hearns tapped gloves, the opening bell sounded, the crowd roared, and the fight between two perfectly matched athletes began.

Ray had spent weeks studying films of Hearns' fights, paying particular attention to the knockouts – which had occurred in 30 of 32 fights. In every case, Ray saw, Hearns' ultimate weapon – indeed, his main weapon – was his right hand. It was like a bomb, and it was devastating. Ray's strategy was to stay out of the way of that right hand, moving and dancing and countering with punches that would hit their mark. His cornerman, Angelo Dundee, concurred with this strategy, and in fact the two had discussed it frequently during the previous two weeks after Dundee, as was his custom, had come on board to put the finishing touches to Ray's training. Dundee had a historic reference, as usual, recalling how Muhammad Ali never got hit in the head because he always pulled back, lessening the force even of a punch that connected. If Ray was successful in avoiding Hearns' 'ultimate weapon', he would make Hearns mad, and this was the second part of Ray's strategy: he was going to try to 'bring out the street' in Hearns, knowing from personal experience that when a fighter reacts in the ring the way he did when he was a kid he loses his composure and forgets about basic boxing essentials.

In Round 1, Ray had trouble carrying out his strategy of

dodging and counter-punching. Hearns, with his longer reach, kept Leonard at bay and denied him the opportunity to go inside. So when the round ended, Ray implemented the second part of his plan. When the bell rang, he tapped Hearns on the forehead and said, 'I gotcha now, turkey!' Predictably, Hearns took a swing at Ray, causing the crowd to boo at this display of bad sportsmanship, and making Hearns even more upset.

The second round began as a replay of the first, with Ray dancing, moving from side to side, shaking his hips, and smiling, but throwing comparatively few punches. On occasion, he threw a jab or released a combination, but he was trying to tire Hearns, who had never gone more than ten rounds in one bout. Then, just before the bell, Hearns caught Ray with a short right, and Ray's left eye, the same one that had been injured two weeks earlier in a sparring session, immediately began to water and swell up. A look of satisfaction passed over Hearns' face, one of resignation over Ray's. In Ray's corner, Angelo Dundee congratulated himself on coming prepared with a special 'do-hickey' for eye injuries. He placed the flat metal disc that had been immersed in a bucket of ice over Ray's eye, and the sharp sting of cold caused the swelling to go down immediately. Dundee couldn't help remembering the Ali–Liston match of 1964 when Ali was blinded, apparently by medication that had been smeared on Liston's bloody cheek. Ali had panicked and wanted to stop the fight, but Dundee had put water in his eyes and told his fighter to run until his eyes cleared. Ray Leonard wasn't panicking. His injury only made him more determined to show what he was made of.

Going into the third round, Ray realized that he must be behind on the judges' scorecards. He needed to get the fight going his way. He started slugging, answering every Hearns right jab with a flurry of counterpunches to the head. At the same time, he dodged and weaved, trying to protect his injured eye and not let Hearns get near it. When the bell rang, he was sure he had won that round.

In the next two rounds, Hearns responded by going

back to basics, working the jab to the body and concentrating on landing as many punches as he could on Leonard's vulnerable left eye. As the eye continued to swell, Hearns decided that the bout would soon be over. All he needed was one good right jab. Then, Ray landed a solid left hook, and Hearns was actually hurt for the first time. Ray saw this, and he, too, decided it was time to put the bout on ice.

In the sixth round, both fighters came out punching. Hearns threw rights, but for every one he landed Ray answered with a staccato of hooks and rights to the head. Ray missed a left but scored with a right to his opponent's jaw. Hearns came back with two jabs to Ray's face. They traded punches for a minute, then Ray scored with two left-right combinations. At the bell, he had driven Hearns to the ropes, and when Hearns wobbled back to his corner on unsteady legs it was clear that he had literally been saved by the bell. When the seventh round began, Hearns was still hurt, and Ray stopped dancing to size up his opponent's condition. Then he attacked with his left. Hearns wobbled but struck back with his right jab. Ray answered with a furious combination that again drove Hearns to the ropes. More combinations from Ray. Hearns looked as if he had lost all his strength, but as the round ended he landed a couple of powerful punches to Ray's body.

Ray won the sixth and seventh rounds by huge margins, but at considerable cost. His arms were tired from throwing so many punches. He was also winded. But he still had the energy to keep baiting Hearns, trying to bring out 'the street in him'.

A new Hearns came out of his corner for the start of the eighth round. More accurately, it was a resurrected Hearns, for beginning in that round he went back to a boxing strategy he hadn't used since his amateur days. He struck and ran, occasionally stopping to throw a limited combination. In response, Ray found himself standing his ground, and more than once cocking a right that he ended up not delivering because Hearns had moved away. It was almost a complete role reversal for the two fighters. Both recognized that fact, and when the bell rang they gave each other a salute, each acknowledging the other's courage. There would be no more late punches and post-bell insults that night.

Meanwhile, the crowd was growing restless. They weren't used to seeing such role reversal. Hearns' fans didn't think much of the dainty tactics being displayed by their hero. By the tenth round, Hearns was being booed, which didn't help his psychological state. But some of the boos were for Sugar Ray, since both used the round essentially to rest and to do more dancing than punching. By this time, more than a few keen observers had noticed that in the 100-degree plus heat, which was at least 20 degrees hotter in the ring because of the TV camera lights, Thomas Hearns was not sweating. So that's how he'd managed to weigh in at 145 pounds – he'd spent a lot of time in the sauna. Even a strong man can only go so long in such a dehydrated state. Ray, who was beginning to get his second wind, had an idea it would not be long before he could finish off Hearns.

In the eleventh round, Hearns was the aggressor, scoring repeatedly with lefts and rights, especially his famous jab. His supporters began to chant 'Tom-ee, Tom-ee', and between rounds he jumped up from his stool and acted as cheerleader. He was unmarked. Over in the opposite corner, Ray's eye was closing fast.

In the twelfth round, Ray tried to regroup. He scored with a left and started to dance. Hearns stalked him, landing a left jab and then connecting, again, with a solid right to Ray's left eye. Ray took three more right jabs from Hearns before landing a good left that drove Hearns backwards. Then Hearns scored with a vicious left to the damaged eye as the round ended. When the bell rang, both fighters just stood and looked at each other for a moment. Then they tapped gloves in a sign of mutual respect.

In Ray's corner, Angelo Dundee worked feverishly on his eye. 'You're blowing, it, kid, you're blowing it!' he yelled, and Ray knew he was right. He was tired and he was worried about his eye, and his fighting showed it. He was going to lose unless he could summon his will to fight on and win. His vision blurred, every muscle in his body aching, he reached deep down inside himself and brought up the guts, the will, that many had questioned even existed.

In the thirteenth round, Ray came out quickly and landed a left jab. He followed with a right that was too short. Hearns stumbled, but the referee ruled that it was not a knockdown. Hearns hardly even used his right. Later, he said it was because Ray was never there. Both fighters were tired now, and they tried to shore up energy by clinching frequently. Ray used these clinches to unleash a fusillade of punches to Hearns' body. Hearns seemed to have forgotten the rudiments of the clinch. Ray managed to see an opening when Hearns dropped his hands. He unleashed a right-lead, left-hook combination that caused Hearns' legs to buckle. Ray then bore in with a series of uppercuts to Hearns' head, ending with a vicious right that connected. Hearns staggered, lost his balance, and fell backwards between the ropes. Again, referee Davey Pearl ruled no knockdown. Hearns recovered quickly and climbed back into the ring, but Ray knocked him again into the ropes. Davey Pearl gave the mandatory eight count and the bell rang to end the round.

Ray came out of his corner like a shot in the fourteenth round and resumed his brutal punishment of his opponent. He was essentially fighting with one eye, but his adrenalin was pumping, and he forgot how tired he was. While Hearns failed to throw even a single punch, Ray unleashed a barrage of blows, and with 1:45 elapsed, referee Davey Pearl stopped the fight.

Some in the crowd had booed the referee's call. Up in the closed circuit television booth, Dr Ferdie Pacheco, who had been Muhammad Ali's road physician for more than a decade, criticized the call and said that Hearns was ahead on points and was capable of continuing the fight. But he later changed his mind after seeing tapes of the contest. When the fight ended, Hearns was still on his feet, but just barely. He fell while trying to negotiate the steps down from the ring.

Back in the ring, Sugar Ray Leonard raised his fist in victory, but he was worrying about his eye and eager to get to his dressing-room so it could be treated. He had less than a quarter of his normal vision out of the eye when the fight ended. Leaving the ring, he had to be supported by two of his aides. Juanita was crying.

Both fighters wore dark glasses to conceal their injuries when they met for the post-fight press conference. With Little Ray sitting at his side and his wife and mother standing behind him, Sugar Ray was elated. It was the toughest fight he had ever fought, he told reporters, and he had to fight from the bottom of his guts to win. He now held two separate WBA boxing titles – both the welterweight and the junior middleweight titles – as well as the WBC welterweight title. A week later he relinquished the WBA junior middleweight title, for WBA rules forbade the holding of two titles simultaneously; but the fact that he had held them simultaneously would still go down in boxing history as a major accomplishment. He was in a position to be generous, but the compliment which he paid to Thomas Hearns at that post-fight press conference was heartfelt. 'We're both champions,' he declared, nodding to his opponent.

Hearns stated his agreement that both were champions. One had to go, and it had been him, but he didn't plan to be gone for long. 'Detroit,' he promised his hometown fans, 'I will return.' Both spent the bulk of the press conference saying respectful things about each other, because they knew, as few others could, just how much courage it had taken to go those thirteen-plus rounds. Indeed, more than one sports writer averred that both men had fought magnificently and that it was their class alone that had elevated the bout from the sheer commercial spectacle it had promised to be to a memorable and worthwhile contest. For Ray, the important thing was that he had preserved his title with a late-round knockout when he was behind on the scorecards of all three judges.

No one could accuse him of having it easy after that fight.

Later on, after sports writers and boxing *aficionados* compared their scoring of the match with that of the three judges, many found it unbelievable that all three judges had Hearns ahead going into the fourteenth round. The majority of sports writers at ringside had scored the bout much closer, and some had Leonard slightly ahead. A few later wrote that Leonard had not been up against one opponent, but five – Hearns, the referee who had refused to count two Hearns falls as knockdowns, and the three judges. Ray's people agreed. They understood that if the fight had gone the full fifteen rounds without a knockout or a technical knockout their man would have lost. Mike Trainer stated publicly that Sugar Ray Leonard would never win a close decision because too many people in boxing resented him, a sentiment that seemed to be supported by the reaction of one judge who, when asked why he had scored certain rounds for Hearns, not Leonard, asked, 'What's the matter, is that little brat complaining?'

The Leonards were soon to feel somebody's resentment. Hardly had they returned to their hotel suite when an anonymous caller threatened to blow them up. They quickly relocated to another hotel, and nothing more was heard from the bomber. Nervously, they realized that they were likely targets for crazies by sheer virtue of Ray's fame.

The fight grossed a reported thirty-six million dollars, making it the richest single sports event in history. Ray took home ten million, Hearns five million. But for Hearns, the money was not enough to assuage a badly bruised ego. In the weeks following the fight his perspective changed considerably, and he insisted that the fight should not have been stopped, that he had never lost control. Not long afterwards, Hearns announced that he wanted a rematch, but Ray was not interested, although he understood Hearns' desire to show he could fight Ray Leonard again and this time beat him. Ray had been bothered by Hearns' later statements about the fight, more than a little annoyed that the man he had beaten would not admit that he had indeed been beaten. Ray Leonard's ego came to the fore with this reaction. Thomas Hearns would get no rematch unless he cried 'Uncle' loud and clear. That never happened. Thus, despite the potential box-office appeal of a rematch between two of the most courageous fighters in the game, the two would not meet in the ring again.

Sugar Ray taunts Duran—and wins the rematch.

A few of the honours and trophies Sugar Ray has received.

Jabbing with the left.

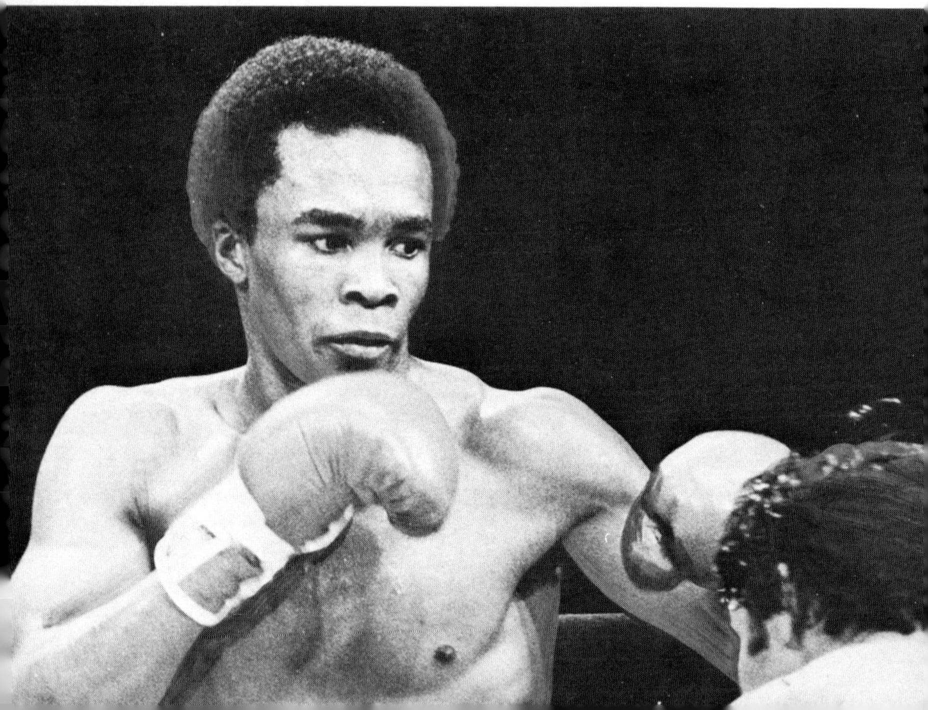

Marvin Hagler ducks from a swing by Sugar Ray.

Sugar Ray watches Donny Lalonde fall to the canvas.

8

Staying on Top

RAY FELT THAT, in terms of money, the fight against Hearns was like the closing chapter of a book – it was the richest bout in boxing history, the richest sporting event in history, and there were really no more financial mountains to conquer. In fact, it was a good time to retire, if he felt in the mood to retire. The idea had crossed his mind. He had never been so badly hurt in a bout as in the Hearns fight. His wife confided that she had been afraid he might never see again. His young son had been frightened, too. The morning following the fight he asked, 'Daddy, why do you keep on fighting? Why don't you take up another sport?' Ray asked him which one, and the little boy replied, 'Like basketball.'

But Ray wasn't prepared to retire at that point. He had no alternative plans for the way to spend the rest of his life. He would stick with boxing until he had something better to do. In the meantime, he would go after another first.

At the time, the only fight Ray could see being worthwhile was a match for a third title. Not since Henry Armstrong won three separate and legitimate titles in three different weight classes had such a thing been done. If he could make middleweight, he could challenge Marvin Hagler's title. Now, that would be box office. It would also be something different. Ray Leonard didn't want to step into a ring again unless there was a real purpose to exposing himself to all that abuse.

Marvelous Marvin Hagler (he'd had his name changed leagally in a Boston court) liked that idea himself. The Brockton, Massachusetts, fighter had held the world middleweight title since September 1980 when he had won the crown from Alan Minter of England, and had successfully defended it three times, the most recent on 3 October 1981, against Mustafa Hamsho. It was his 53rd win, bringing his professional record to 53-2-2, and his 28th consecutive win since a ten-round loss to Willie Monroe in Philadelphia in 1976. It was also his 44th knockout. Hagler sported a shaved head and a mean visage, and the day after his victory over Hamsho he announced that he wanted to fight Leonard.

About thirteen pounds stood between the two fighters, however. Hagler refused to fight Leonard at the 154-pound, junior middleweight limit, stating that Leonard would have to hit the 160-pound middleweight mark on the scale. Ray realized that thirteen pounds would make a significant difference in his game, for as a general rule the more weight a fighter puts on, the less effective he is in the ring. He was not about to rush into middleweight contention. Instead, he decided to test the waters in the heavier divisions first.

A further barrier to a Leonard–Hagler fight was that Hagler was still under contract to promoter Bob Arum, with whom Trainer and Leonard had refused to do business since a misunderstanding over the Kalule fight. It was rumoured that Hagler was trying to get free of Arum, but until that happened there would be no serious negotiations between the Leonard and Hagler camps.

While Ray had no big fights or big purses to look forward to, at least for the time being, he still had to fight. Not only did he need regular bouts to keep him psychologically and physically in training, the WBA and WBC required periodic defences of titles. Both organizations had already presented Leonard's people with a list of potential challengers. Trainer got busy lining up Ray's agenda for the following year. In February, he would fight Bruce Finch, who had been stopped in three rounds by Thomas Hearns. Next, Trainer hoped to get a bout against Roger Stafford, a Philadelphian who had recently upset Pipino Cuevas. Assuming that Leonard won that bout, Trainer was eyeing Chung Hwae-Chang of South

Korea, who was rated by the WBA ahead of Hearns, for a summer match. And in the autumn, he was thinking of getting a bout for Ray with Alexis Arguello, the WBC lightweight champion, or with Roger Pryor, the undefeated WBA junior welterweight champion and the Number 1 ranked WBC welterweight. Much of this agenda depended on how these potential opponents fared over the next few months.

Ray's first defence of his world welterweight championship was against Bruce Finch in Reno on 15 February. Finch, a black, a native of Milwaukee, Wisconsin, who fought out of Las Vegas, had won eleven straight victories since he was knocked out in the second round of a bout against Thomas Hearns on 7 September 1978. With a record of 28-3-1, he was ranked Number 4 by the WBC, but he was Number 4 on an unexciting list. In fact, the list of welterweight contenders was so dismal that there was not, in actuality, a good deal of difference between Number 1 and Number 10. During his career, Finch had been beaten by Pete Ranzany and Larry Bonds in five rounds as well as by Thomas Hearns. Ray had knocked out all three of them. Gamblers wouldn't even bet on Finch to win, so odds-makers had to concentrate on whether Leonard would stop him before or after the eighth round.

Nobody was going to get rich off ticket sales to this bout, the first championship match held in Reno since the Jack Johnson–Jim Jeffries fight in 1910, so Trainer and Finch's representative made a deal with cable television's 'Home Box Office' to broadcast the fight live. That brought the purse for Leonard to a level that he could accept without embarrassment – $1.3 million. The $85,000 promised to Finch, according to Pat Putnam of *Sports Illustrated*, was 'about $82,000 more than he had ever earned for a bout'.

Ray trained for the fight as if his crown was actually on the line. He understood that this was the opportunity of a lifetime for Finch, and he wasn't going to make a mistake by getting careless. At the weekend news conference, Ray first predicted that the fight would not go past eight rounds, then, when Finch claimed he would put Leonard 'on the deck', changed his prediction: 'Four rounds, now,' he said. Minutes before the bout was to start, he had completed a good warm-up and his timing was perfect. Then, someone from Home Box Office arrived to say there were technical difficulties and there would be a slight delay to the start of the match. Ray cooled off, and went cold. When word came that the technical difficulties had been solved, he tried to warm up again, but there wasn't time for a proper warm-up before the TV cameras were ready for the show to go on.

'Run,' Angelo Dundee and Janks Morton said, and as soon as he entered the ring Ray dutifully began circling his opponent quickly, trying to warm up as the bout began. But he couldn't get into the match. His timing was off. He felt as if everything was operating in slow motion. Finch connected with a solid right to the body in that first round, but it didn't wake up Leonard.

Between rounds, Ray heard his cornermen advise him to step up his pace. Back in the ring, he danced more quickly, baiting his opponent, daring Finch to come after him. Suddenly, he slowed his pace, and Finch connected with a combination to his head. Ray was dazed. Finch had hurt him – worse, he said later, than either Roberto Duran or Wilfred Benitez had hurt him. That punch woke him up to the fact that he was in a real fight. Quickly, he backed into a corner, knowing that Finch would follow him there and get in close. He realized that he'd have to get him in the corners because he could not reach him in the middle of the ring. He did not have the snap in the jab that he'd expected to have. Before the round was over, Ray had landed a left hook to Finch's body that caused him to bend over in pain, and followed it with two more hooks, one of which connected with his head. A hard right, and Finch was on the canvas. Mills Lane, the referee, began the count, stopping at nine. Finch staggered to his feet. During the count, Ray had willed Finch to remain down. He wanted out of this fight. He wasn't in tune. Besides, the night before he'd dreamed of knocking down an opponent who never got up. But Finch wasn't cooperating, and Ray reluctantly went after him again, unleashing a flurry of blows. Finch went down again, this time for a count of seven. He held on until the bell rang.

In Round 3, Finch came out smoking, but he was no match for Ray, even when his timing was off. Left uppercuts combined with straight rights drove Finch to his knees. The referee counted nine, and Finch staggered to his feet, but he was so unsteady that he fell back against the ropes. Now Mills stepped in to end the fight. Time elapsed in the third round was one minute, fifty seconds.

The fight would hardly go down in the record books, and the win was no cause for rejoicing in the Leonard camp. Ordinarily, Ray's father, Morton, Dundee and Trainer would talk about a fight afterwards. This time, on the trip back to the hotel, there was silence. Later, Ray confided to Juanita that he was again thinking about quitting the fight game, but Juanita was sceptical. Neither of them said anything to others.

For Ray, there was little time to ponder the future, because he was soon training for his next bout, against Roger Stafford in May. Stafford had won an upset victory over Pipino Cuevas the previous November, earning a place in the top ten WBC contenders. Oddly enough, that had not caused the WBC to alter the rankings much – according to the next rating list released, Cuevas was still Number 1, with Stafford as Number 4. Nevertheless, Jose Sulaiman, president of the WBC, approved a Leonard–Stafford fight for May.

Inevitably, there were the questions about a possible bout against Hagler, but the story was essentially the same. Hagler wouldn't come down in weight, at least not enough to satisfy Leonard and his people. How important weight was and how fine a line could be drawn over weight was indicated by a statement Trainer made to a writer for *Sports Illustrated* at the time. 'People accuse us of ducking Hagler. They think it's a matter of a few pounds. Heck, we'll fight Hagler at 160 if he agrees to weigh in at 160 on his way into the ring. But if he weighs in at 160 in the morning, he'll come in at 167 or 168 that night. Ray will weigh 154. All we're trying to do, if they want to fight us, is narrow the gap in weight difference between Rounds 5 and 12 where it really counts.'

With the Hagler fight still up in the air, Ray Leonard's people went about negotiating contracts for the forthcoming fight against Stafford. It was decided to stage the bout in Buffalo, in the western part of New York state, where unemployment exceeded 12 per cent and an influx of fight dollars would do much for the city's ailing economy. To make the fight worthwhile for Ray, his representatives negotiated with ABC-TV to broadcast live from the War Memorial Coliseum in Buffalo.

In late April Ray and his entourage set up camp near Buffalo for intensive training for his bout against Stafford. Ray was feeling anything but intense; in fact, he later described himself as 'in neutral'. He was in a lousy mood and kept to himself most of the time, playing video games in a room next to his bedroom or watching movies. Working out became a chore. Then he began to complain to Janks Morton that his left eye wasn't quite right. When he got up in the morning, he would see a flash of light in that eye, although it would go away. Then, after roadwork, he occasionally saw a black dot in front of his left eye. Also, if he tried to focus on an object the eye would feel sore, and Morton took him to a physician in Buffalo, who prescribed eye drops and rest. Ray dutifully applied the eye drops, and even wore dark glasses in order to rest the eye. Meanwhile, he continued training, but about two weeks before the bout against Stafford he broke training and went home for the weekend. He took Juanita and his mother out to dinner and ate a pile of pasta and drank wine. He had never done that while in serious training before. He didn't even run while he was home. He started out on a run with his two security guards, Irving Millard and Craig Jones, but after about a mile and half he slowed to a walk. When they asked him what was wrong, he said, 'Man, I'm tired of this. I just don't want it any more. After this fight I'm going to quit.'

Not even the prospect of a fight against Aaron Pryor could get his adrenalin going. Pryor, perhaps in an effort to get a bout with Ray, had been telling reporters that Ray owed him, because they had been friends and Ray hadn't helped him. That galled Ray, who has said, 'That's the reason friends don't work for me – they're always expecting you to do them favours. It's difficult to have friends and family working for you.' He would have liked nothing better than to put a fist in Pryor's mouth to shut him up, but he still wasn't feeling ready for another bout, even against Pryor.

Back in Buffalo, during a routine sparring match, Ray took a punch to the right side of his head. The punch was not even hard, but he had put some drops into his eye before the workout and he was very aware of it. He began to back away from the blow, more self-conscious than he should have been about being hit. Then a glob of Albolene cream dropped from his headgear on to his right eyelid, and Ray became so frightened about losing the vision in his right eye that he abruptly ended the bout and went to his room for the rest of the day. Two days later, when his left eye still bothered him, a second doctor was consulted. This one said there was a tear in the retina and that it should be taken care of immediately. This news was serious. Next to brain damage, a detached retina is the worst injury a fighter can have.

Fighters are not the only athletes who suffer from that injury. In 1980, 2,600 tennis players and 2,100 racquetball players, as well as 2,100 boxers were treated for eye injuries of all types. A sharp blow to the eye can often knock the retina loose, so that it floats into the vitreous body, the transparent mass of soft, gelatinous material that makes up most of the eye organ. Normally, the retina, which is a paper-thin transparent membrane, is firmly attached towards the front of the eye and at the optic nerve. Elsewhere, it adheres only lightly. When it becomes detached from one of those two anchor sites, it must be operated on quickly. Otherwise, blindness will result.

A number of fighters had been forced to retire because of this injury, among them Harold Weston, Jr, who suffered a detached retina in a welterweight bout with Thomas Hearns in 1979 and subsequently retired to become a matchmaker for Madison Square Garden. In earlier days, there had been no operation possible, and so a fighter like Wesley Mouzon never fought again after suffering a detached retina in the eighth round of a WBC lightweight title fight against Bob Montgomery in 1946. Many years later, Leotis Matin beat Sonny Liston when Liston was trying to make a comeback. It was the biggest win of Matin's life, but he damaged the retina of one eye and never fought again.

With the advent of microsurgery, a detached retina did not automatically signal retirement, however. Former heavyweight contender Earnie Shavers had suffered a detached retina when he was knocked out by Larry Holmes in a 1979 heavyweight title bout. The fight had been stopped in the eleventh round because of Shavers' injury, which at first had been reported as a wound requiring only stitches due to Shavers' getting 'thumbed' in the third round. Later, after the injury was correctly diagnosed as a detached retina, Shavers was successfully operated on by Dr Ronald G. Michels, associate professor of ophthalmology at Johns Hopkins Hospital's Wilmer Eye Institute. Shavers was scheduled to fight Joe Bugner in Dallas in early May.

Janks Morton remembered that Shavers had had surgery at Johns Hopkins Hospital in Baltimore, and Ray was relieved to know that there was a specialist near his home. While Dunlap made plane reservations for Morton, Ray and Ray's father to return to Baltimore the following day, Morton got in touch with Mike Trainer and asked him to find out the name of the surgeon who had operated on Shavers. Trainer called Dr Henry Starr, of Riverdale, Maryland, who had treated Ray after he suffered a trauma to his right eye in a fight against Marcos Geraldo in 1979, and got the name of the specialist, Dr Ronald Michels. He scheduled an appointment for Ray as soon as he arrived from Buffalo the following day.

The next day, Saturday, Trainer sent a limousine to pick up Juanita Leonard, and the two met at the airport to wait for Ray and his father to arrive. Then, they all went to Johns Hopkins Hospital.

Michels' diagnosis was that Ray had a partially detached retina and that his injury was less serious than

Shavers' had been. However, he required an operation immediately. Ray, Juanita, Cicero Leonard, Janks Morton and Mike Trainer adjourned to a small room to discuss the matter of when the operation should take place. Juanita began to sob, but the attitude of the men was simply to get it over with. They decided to have the operation done the following day, Sunday, since by Monday reporters would have got wind of the problem and the place would be swarming with them.

Ray was admitted that night. Juanita stayed with him, making arrangements with her mother, Geraldine Savoy, to have Little Ray stay with a friend. The following morning, Getha Leonard arrived to give her son a good luck kiss before he went into surgery. Meanwhile, Geraldine Savoy was on her way to Baltimore with Little Ray, who had not yet been told about his father. When he learned that his father was undergoing an operation on his eye, he cried himself to sleep in the car.

Later that morning, Ray underwent two hours of surgery performed by a three-doctor team led by Michels. The doctors reattached about 40 per cent of the retinal tissue behind Ray's left eye. The prognosis was good for complete recovery; but neither Michels nor Ray's representative would speak about the future. 'It's all up to the individual,' said Michels at a post-operation news conference, adding that while retinal surgery was successful 90 per cent of the time, it would take several weeks to determine whether or not this particular operation had been a success. While Dr Michels did not refer to Earnie Shavers, it was not lost on observers that almost as he spoke, Shavers was knocking out Bugner in Windsor, Ontario, making good on his gamble to risk the vision in one eye for another shot at the big money he had never made. Boxing historians also pointed out that Maurice Hope of England, a former world light-middleweight champion, had come back from detached retina surgery in 1980 and fought four times before retiring.

Meanwhile, the boxing world was waiting with bated breath. Injuries currently plagued that world. The cancellation of the Leonard–Stafford bout was the second title defence to be pushed back in a single week, and the third in the previous two months. Earlier in the week, Marvin Hagler's middleweight title defence against Thomas Hearns scheduled for 24 May in Windsor, Ontario, had been postponed due to an injury to one of Hearns' little fingers. Back in early March, Larry Holmes' WBC heavyweight title defence against Gerry Cooney, scheduled for the 15th of the month in Las Vegas, had been put off until 11 June after Cooney had suffered a shoulder injury.

Within days after Leonard's surgery, a fourth major title fight had to be postponed because of an injury. This time, Mike Weaver, who was to have defended the WBA heavyweight title on 2 June against Randall (Tex) Cobb, hurt his shoulder lifting weights in training. The fight, scheduled for Atlantic City's Convention Hall, was called off.

Needless to say, there was considerable consternation in the fight world. In the case of the Leonard–Stafford fight, the cancellation meant about $2 million in lost revenue for the city of Buffalo including refunds for tickets that had been sold for about 14,000 of the 18,000 seats in War Memorial Coliseum.

ABC-TV suddenly had two hours of programming to fill. Marvin Hagler, not to mention other fighters who were in the running to meet Sugar Ray Leonard down the line, faced the loss of hefty meal tickets. But the fighters, at least, had their priorities in the right place when they made public statements about Ray's operation. Faced themselves with the constant risk of serious injury, they understood the difficulty of the decision Ray would eventually have to make, *if* his eye healed completely. Said Stafford, 'I wouldn't fight, I wouldn't risk my eye. Ray's made it. He shouldn't fight anymore.'

Naturally, there was speculation about how Ray received the injury, particularly about whether or not Thomas Hearns was the cause. But Dr Michels said it was impossible to tell when and in what circumstances the injury had occurred. It could have started with the sparring mishap before the Hearns fight. It could also have occurred during recent sparring sessions.

Meanwhile, the object of all this speculation was recuperating nicely, and deluged by well-wishers. Telegrams and telephone calls from as far away as Sweden and Argentina poured into Johns Hopkins University Medical Center, which had to set up a special communications centre to handle all the inquiries about Ray and to screen calls. One call that was allowed to go through was from President Ronald Reagan, calling from Chicago where he had addressed a group of editors and visited a predominantly black Catholic school. Another was from Ray's old nemesis, Roberto Duran. Someone sent a four-leafed clover picked in 1887. A terminally ill cancer patient in Puerto Rico wrote and offered Ray his eyes. Ray was touched by these expressions of support and generosity.

Ray went home from the hospital on Monday, 16 May, surrounded by a dozen security guards carrying bouquets of flowers. According to his doctors, he was in 'excellent' condition and they saw no reason why he should not be at home to celebrate his twenty-sixth birthday the following day. They refused to speculate about his long-term prognosis or about his return to boxing. Ironically, at the same time as Ray was going home from the hospital, it was announced that WBC lightweight challenger, Lotte Mwale, had been forced to postpone his 27 May bout with champion Dwight Braxton due to an eye injury suffered while sparring.

Sugar Ray Leonard intended to take time to make his decision. There was no pressure on him to make any choices right away. A spokesman for the World Boxing Council in Mexico City said that if Ray wanted to fight again, he would get all the time he needed to prepare for his title defence. Bob Lee, a vice-president of the World Boxing Association, said that the WBA would grant Ray six months or more before requiring a title defence.

What Ray did not know was whether fate would grant him the full restoration of his eyesight. True, 90-95 per cent of retinal reattachment operations were successful in terms of anatomical repair. But visual repair rates varied greatly, according to the specifics of the damage in each case. Of the 25,000 cases each year, about 4,000 recovered full vision and another 16,000 recovered some vision. But, of these, about 6,000 recovered only a small part of their vision and some became legally blind.

Janks Morton was certain that Ray would return to the ring and said as much to a reporter in an ill-advised interview. The next day sports pages around the country reported that there was 'no question' that Ray would return to the ring and that his next fight would be in February. That made it necessary for Ray to issue a statement through his PR man, Charles Brotman, that no decision had been made about his return. 'No announcement will be made until my eye is completely healed, which should be several months from now,' the statement read, 'and when an announcement is made, I will personally make it.'

Ray made his first public appearance on 26 May at a news conference at the International Hotel in Washington, DC. He was wearing spectacles, which he said were made of plain glass and which he had borrowed from his brother Kenny to serve as protection from dirt or small objects. His left eye was visibly bloodshot, although he assured reporters that it was healing well. Asked about a possible return to the ring, he reiterated that he would defer his decision until the eye was completely healed. He admitted that his wife, Juanita, was more determined than ever that he should retire, but he would have to follow his own heart. If his eye did heal completely, then he would have to decide whether the itch to compete was still too strong to allow him to retire. He agreed that he didn't need to return to boxing for the money or for the ego-gratification. The crucial issue would be how he felt about being in the ring. He related to reporters how frightened he had been when he thought both his eyes were in trouble during the routine sparring match while he was training for the Stafford fight. He had backed away from a punch in order to protect his eye. He knew he could not go into a fight without being prepared to go all out, forgetting about possible injury. He would retire in a minute if he sensed fear in himself.

That summer, Ray went on a cruise aboard the QE2 to make a documentary film for a Canadian company. For a lark, he agreed to spar with a young member of the ship's crew who had fought as both an amateur and a pro. His opponent was 6 ft 1 in and 185 pounds and wore 12-ounce gloves. Ray wore 8-ounce gloves. It was supposed to be a casual match, but all the people aboard gathered to watch, and for Ray the old killer instinct began to come out once his young opponent's taps started knocking him halfway across the ring. He went for the kid, and dropped him with a kidney shot. Later, he asked himself how he could have been so stupid as to have sparred with anyone so soon after his operation.

Back home, Ray signed contracts to do sports commentating for Home Box Office and for CBS-TV and agreed to do promotional spots for Franklin Sporting Goods. But that still left about two weeks out of each month for him to spend at home, and he enjoyed the opportunity to be with Juanita and Little Ray. He also enjoyed not feeling the pressure of staying in training in order to be ready for his next fight. He kept himself in shape, but he did not miss serious training.

In fact, life was sweet for Sugar Ray except for one nagging problem – wherever he went, people asked about his eye and whether or not he would fight again. For months, he had been answering that his eye was getting better. By the autumn, he had started responding sullenly, 'It's the same way.' He purposely did roadwork in public, and even sparred a couple of times to let people know that he was keeping in shape. In October, he visited Dr Ronald Michels who told him that although it usually took six months to see if the retina had been fully reattached, Ray's was almost perfectly healed. Michels gave Ray the green light to fight again.

Now, it was up to Ray whether or not he re-entered the ring, and he had little trouble making his decision. He was twenty-six years old, in his prime, and he was going to retire. 'I simply don't want to fight any more,' he told reporters. He went on to say that he believed he would have retired after the Stafford fight anyway, and the injury had made his decision to retire that much easier. He'd defeated all the big names in his weight categories, and was left with uninspiring opponents, fights over which he simply could not get excited.

He admitted that he had been essentially play-acting for the past six months and knew in his heart that he was going to retire. He regretted having led the public on. But he did not want it to appear as if the eye injury had KO'd him. He was retiring because he wanted to, not because he had been forced to. And so, as of 9 November 1982, Sugar Ray Leonard was a fighter no more. As he put it, the final chapter of Sugar Ray Leonard the fighter had been written. The book was closed.

9

Ray Unretires

EXACTLY ONE WEEK after Ray announced his retirement, in a televised fight from Miami, Aaron Pryor knocked Alexis Arguello senseless. He lay unconscious on the canvas for four long minutes before coming around, and the world held its breath. For Ray Leonard, it was a sign that he had made the right decision, for it might have been him in the ring with Pryor. Although he believed that he could have beaten Pryor if they had met as originally planned in the autumn of 1982, he realized that he was lucky to have the luxury of such speculation without being put to the test.

The night following the Pryor–Arguello bout, South Korean Duk-Koo Kim was not so lucky. After a fourteenth-round TKO by Ray 'Boom Boom' Macini in a lightweight championship bout in las Vegas, Duk-Koo Kim collapsed and had to be carried from the ring on a stretcher. He underwent surgery for removal of a 100-cc blood clot, but died five days later without ever regaining consciousness. Films of the fight showed that during one fifty-second period in the thirteenth round, he had taken thirty-nine punches, most of them to the head, and yet according to the surgeon who operated on him, the fatal blood clot was caused by a single punch that landed later, because the haemorrhage was fresh.

The fight had been televised as part of CBS's show '*Sports Saturday*', and thus many more people besides serious fight fans witnessed the bout, and the fatal blow. For some, it was the last boxing match they ever watched, so great was the revulsion over the blood sport.

Around the same time, the public learned that Muhammad Ali was suffering from Parkinson's disease, a disorder of the central nervous system. That explained the mumbling, the slurring of words, the almost classic personification of the stereotype of the punch-drunk fighter. Although doctors would not definitely attribute the disease to the blows Ali had received in the ring, there was no question in the public mind that boxing was to blame.

All this gave Ray Leonard pause. He had suggested once before that his eye injury had been 'a sign from God'. Now, he was even more firmly convinced that he had got out of boxing just in time. The unfortunate thing for boxing was that in losing Sugar Ray Leonard it had also lost one of the few attractive, clean, likeable practitioners of the sport.

Juanita Leonard and Little Ray were even more sure than Ray that he had retired just in time. They were delighted to have their husband and father back with them, and in good shape. In return for her husband keeping his promise, Juanita kept one she had made to him: they could now have more children. He'd spoken often of having more, but each time she had declared that there was no point in having another child until such time as he would be around to devote proper attention to it, until they could be a real family. About a year later, Juanita announced that she was indeed pregnant.

Now that they were expecting another child, Ray and Juanita decided they needed a larger house, and in the autumn of 1983 they moved into their third home in less than four years of marriage. This one was more fitting for a millionaire former athlete – a million-dollar, seven-bedroom mini-mansion of brick, with a stone turret on two and a half acres in Potomac, Maryland, one of the more fashionable suburbs of Washington, DC. Ray, who now had time to devote to such things, was deeply involved in the decoration of the house.

He was quite content. He was enjoying the opportunity to develop his skill as a sports commentator for television, and was concentrating on being a real professional, as opposed to an athlete who just happened to do 'colour' at occasional athletic contests. He was also entertaining offers from Hollywood to appear in films. It was a delight to be able to go to bed and get up when he wanted to, to eat what he wanted to, to be able to call his time his own, to concentrate on less physically taxing sports like tennis and golf.

But part of his heart still belonged to boxing. When he did ringside commentary for Home Box Office (his contract with CBS was not renewed), he could feel the old surge inside, particularly when one of the fighters was someone like Aaron Pryor or Marvin Hagler. He kept thinking that he could beat them.

What also interested him greatly was the formation in 1983 of a third world boxing organization, the Newark, New Jersey-based International Boxing Federation. With three different titles in each weight class in contention at any one time, there would be a plethora of potential opponents who were worth their ranking, or so it was hoped. Moreover, the formation of the IBF showed clearly that boxing, for all its infamy, was still alive and well and ready to command big purses.

Ray was aware that he had some problems with his right eye, not the one that had been operated on, and he studied his old training films, trying to see if he did something to make himself more vulnerable to injury. He concluded that it was during a sparring session that he suffered the detached retina. Somehow, that conclusion made him feel that boxing in the ring was not dangerous for him.

And then a thumbless boxing glove was developed. This was a particular boon, for most eye problems were caused by thumbs stuck in the eyes. Both the WBA and the WBC agreed that such gloves could be worn in the ring. Moreover, Ray realized that wearing thumbless gloves in sparring matches would cut down greatly on the possibilities of injuries to his eyes.

As the months of retirement wore on, he found himself beginning to work out, not just running in the morning, but skipping and shadow-boxing. By the autumn of 1983 he was even doing some sparring, always with the new thumbless gloves. Juanita Leonard was aware of this increased boxing activity, but she said nothing.

In November 1983, Ray scheduled three two-round exhibition fights for mid-December at Andrew Air Force Base outside Washington, DC. When he asked his son how he felt about his participating in the exhibition, Little Ray's response was very perceptive: 'Dad, don't do it. Because if you do, and look good, you'll want to make a comeback.' Weighing 151 pounds and wearing thumbless gloves, he dropped light heavyweight Herman Epps with a right cross in the third round and then walked through three rounds with middleweight Odell Leonard, the former sparring partner who had defected to the Hearns camp. Then, he called a press conference for the following day.

Meanwhile, Juanita Leonard had gone to the hospital with extreme nausea brought on by her pregnancy. When she asked why Ray had to go to another press conference, he told her it was for the reporters who had missed the press conference for the exhibition. But that wasn't the truth. He had called the second press conference to announce that he was coming back out of retirement. He hadn't told Juanita because he was afraid if he did she would talk him out of it. Once he made his announcement publicly, it would be too late to turn back.

Returning to the hospital to tell Juanita that he was going to make a comeback, Ray was astonished when all she said was, 'I knew you would.' There she was, pregnant with the child that she had refused to have until he retired, and there he was coming out of retirement. But Juanita Leonard wanted most of all for her husband to be happy, and so she did not give him an argument. Perhaps in gratitude, he took her on a trip to Nassau, in the Bahamas, for New Year.

Ray planned to launch his comeback in February, against either a ranked welterweight or a junior middleweight, then to go after one of the welterweight champions. If he won one of those titles, he might defend it against the young Welshman Colin Jones. After that, he would move up to junior middleweight and fight Aaron Pryor, or Thomas Hearns, or Roberto Duran, who was back in boxing and re-establishing his reputation as a mauler whose performance in the second Leonard match had been an aberration. Finally, there might actually be the long talked-about fight with Marvelous Marvin Hagler. But Ray would leave all that up to Mike Trainer. His concentration had to be on getting back into real fighting shape both physically and mentally. Not long after his announcement, he went out and bought a candy-apple red Ferrari, and joked that it was to let his future opponents know that he still had some speed.

But he had promised Juanita to be at home more often than he had before. Mike Trainer had sometimes scheduled him too tightly between pre-fight training, fights, and personal appearances. With Juanita having a complicated pregnancy, he knew it would be unfair of him to be away so much that, as she had occasionally told him, she forgot what he looked like.

The boxing world greeted Ray's announcement with great pleasure. Offers to fight poured into Mike Trainer's office, for Sugar Ray Leonard was still the top money-maker and box-office draw in the fight game. Ray told an interviewer for *Ebony*, 'Everybody wants a piece of me. Right now, I'm more important than the title. The guy that beats me would be bigger than boxing, and who wouldn't want to see that on his resumé?' A bout against Kevin Howard was scheduled for 25 February 1984, in Worcester, Massachusetts, and in early January after he and Juanita returned from Nassau Ray went into serious training.

He'd come a long way since his amateur days at the Palmer Park Recreation Center. The gym where he worked out, a former disco right across the street from the old Center, was called the Sugar Ray Leonard Boxing Center. When he ran, his route took him along Sugar Ray Leonard Road (formerly 84th Avenue), a couple of blocks away. But there were some things that were still the same, among them the people who surrounded him. The gym was pungent with the aroma of hot-dogs sold by Mrs Dave Jacobs, wearing a T-shirt inscribed, 'God Bless Sugar Ray', and none other than Jacobs himself was coaching Ray's sparring partners. Ray had invited his old trainer back when he had decided to come out of retirement, and

Jacobs had been eager to re-establish a working relationship with the man he'd practically helped raise. Whatever problems that had existed were smoothed over, and Jacobs remained with Ray from then on.

Ray's right eye bothered him somewhat, but he chose not to have it checked out. Two weeks before the scheduled fight, however, he learned that he would have no choice. The Massachusetts Athletic Commission had adopted new rules mandating pre-fight eye examinations for all contenders, and Ray had to submit to an examination by Dr Edward Ryan of the Eye and Ear Infirmary of Massachusetts General Hospital. Dr Ryan passed Ray's left eye, but found what were described as 'scars and tears' on his right retina. Without treatment, Ray would not be allowed to fight Kevin Howard.

The fight was postponed until such time as Ray was capable of entering a ring. When he heard the news, Kevin Howard said simply, 'If his eye is bad and he can't fight, then God bless him. I have to step on. If we don't fight, give me another opponent.'

Juanita Leonard was less sanguine. She was going through an exceptionally difficult pregnancy, having been in and out of the hospital with bouts of extreme nausea since her second month. She had also developed Bell's Palsy, which had paralyzed one side of her face and which her doctors linked to her condition. Although she was assured that with time and medication the paralysis would diminish, she did not feel up to worrying about her husband when she was so worried about herself and her unborn child. But she did not ask Ray to bow out of a scheduled fight and prayed that his right eye problem was as minor as he assured her it was.

Ray and his advisers consulted Dr Michels at Johns Hopkins, who had known of the condition of Ray's right eye for two years and who had not considered the 'abnormal areas' a threat. Then, after consultations between Dr Michels and Dr Ryan, Dr Ryan performed a relatively simple, five-minute procedure under local anaesthetic called cryotherapy, in which he used a small freezing probe to create adhesion around weak areas of the retina. Having pronounced the treatment successful, Ryan said that Ray ought to be able to resume training in about ten days. But he also advised Ray to quit boxing, saying that he was against boxing in general.

The newspaper headlines seemed to be trying to propel Ray into another retirement, announcing, 'Leonard Advised to Quit Fighting' when Dr Michels at Johns Hopkins was saying that Ray could return to the ring without worry. Mike Trainer, for one, was furious at the way the press was handling the situation, noting that many papers had used the term 'surgery' when the word 'treatment' would have been less hyperbolic. Ray Leonard also resented the comparison made by some reporters of the problems in his eyes, calling the right eye problem a 'baby detached retina'. He chose to listen to Dr Michels, and within days he announced that the fight against Howard would go on. After his follow-up examination, Dr Ryan pronounced him healed and ready to fight.

Ray was thus free to pursue what he hoped would be a careful, steady climb to a new boxing height, although for the time being the end of the rainbow would not be a bout against Marvelous Marvin Hagler. Ray stated publicly around this time that he would no longer consider fighting in a bout promoted by Bob Arum, who was still promoting Hagler's fights exclusively. Ray did not know what eventual goal he might set for himself. For the time being, he only wanted to concentrate on his fight against Kevin Howard, which had been rescheduled for 10 May.

On the morning of 10 May, Ray tipped the scales at 149 pounds. That evening, after his usual light dinner, he weighed 156, four pounds more than normal, and that surprised and bothered him. This was an unusual weight gain, and he worried that it would slow him down, make him sluggish. But he knew he was not facing a major opponent. Howard, a tough Philadelphia fighter, had lost two of his last four bouts and was not even rated by the three boxing organizations. In fact, the fight should be a piece of cake.

That night, Ray pranced into the Worcester Centrum wearing tassels on his black boxing shoes. He smiled and shadow-boxed during the national anthem sung by his sister, Sandra, and when it ended he slammed his red thumbless gloves together in applause. Howard wore thumbless gloves as well, a condition of Ray's fighting him, and this was the first major fight with the new gloves. Three potential opponents were at ringside, and as they stepped into the ring one by one Ray acknowledged them – a polite nod to WBA welterweight champion Donald Curry, a stare at Aaron Pryor, the IBF junior welterweight title holder, a quick bow to Marvin Hagler, the undisputed world middleweight champion. Ray was enjoying the preliminaries and just being back in a ring again. When the bell sounded for Round 1, he smiled at Howard and came on with his hands low in contempt for his opponent's ability to land a punch.

Not long into that round, however, he realized he was not prepared either physically or mentally for the fight. He moved around a lot and tried to establish a rhythm, but was unsuccessful. Later, he recalled that he said to himself, 'Damn, I'm in trouble.' He tried in masterly fashion to cover up for it, and in the third round wound up as if to throw a windmill right hand, then flashed a left jab – one of the moves that had caused Roberto Duran to plead '*No mas*'. More obvious to the audience was his concern with protecting his eyes, for in spite of his attempts to block out the publicity the constant public attention on the condition of his eyes had affected him. During the first three rounds he was visibly protective, ducking his head when he threw his right, pulling his head back as he threw a hook.

By the fourth round, he was aware of what he was doing and tried not to pull back, but in a moment of sloppy defence he allowed Howard to connect – with a sharp right to the chin that knocked him to the floor. Later, Angelo Dundee said, 'I warned Ray not to throw no lazy jab at this guy.' It was Sugar Ray Leonard's first knock-down in his entire pro career, and it was a shock. Up by the count of three, Ray looked over to Juanita, eight months pregnant, who was as shocked as he was. Later, he said that it was at that moment that he knew he had made a mistake in trying to come out of retirement. He had faced major punchers like Roberto Duran and Thomas Hearns and had never been knocked down. Now here was this fourth-rate fighter. . . .

In his corner after the fourth round, Ray tried to listen to Angelo Dundee's advice, but his own thoughts intruded. He had to win. He had been humiliated, but he couldn't let that get to him. He had to finish the fight in style. As he stood before the start of the fifth round, he looked over at Juanita and his mother, and smiled.

For the next two rounds, Ray stayed on his toes, moving and jabbing. Then, in the seventh, he went flat-footed and began to jab, to hook, to uppercut. None of his combinations was working, so he went with single shots, most of which connected. This was the fighting Sugar Ray in action, the wild animal released at last. By the ninth round, Howard was clearly in trouble and with less than a minute remaining Ray snapped Howard's head back with a left hook. Howard grabbed and wrestled him across the ring. Trying to break free, Ray put his left glove under Howard's chin and pushed him away, then followed with two hard rights to the head. After five more punches, none of which connected, referee Richard Flaherty stopped the fight. Under Massachusetts rules, Flaherty could have given Howard a standing eight count to give him time to regain his senses, but he chose not to and instead wrapped his arms around Howard literally to stop him from fighting. Moments later, Sugar Ray Leonard was declared the victor by a TKO.

At the post-fight press conference, Ray faced photographers with a lump on his forehead, a mouse under his right eye where he had been laced, a sprained right wrist and a sore right hip. He had intended to go home and rest for a few days and then announce his retirement, but at the last minute he decided to get the whole thing over with. 'As of this moment, I am retired,' he said simply, explaining that his confidence was not there any more. He looked beaten, and Juanita Leonard's heart went out to her husband. With tears in her eyes, she took the microphone. 'I just want to say that it takes a hell of a man to stand up and admit that. I don't care what anybody says or writes. He's a hell of a man.'

But it was not the way Ray Leonard had imagined his retirement. Kevin Howard was telling reporters that Ray Leonard couldn't hit and that he hadn't really beaten Howard, that he'd been given the win as a 'gift'. Boxing pundits were wondering aloud why Ray was quitting when rustiness was normal for a comeback fighter. Why, back in 1955 Sugar Ray Robinson had come back after two years and had lost a ten-round decision to Ralph (Tiger) Jones. But he had kept fighting. Later that year, at the age of thirty-four, he had won the world middleweight championship away from Carl (Bobo) Olson. But Sugar Ray Leonard had always been a different kind of fighter, and what's more, unlike Robinson, he had undergone eye surgery, and he didn't need the money. Some boxing fans and reporters felt he showed great class. Angelo Dundee was among them. When Ray announced that he would not fight again, Dundee had let out an audible, 'Amen'. Even Kevin Howard later apologized to Ray for saying he couldn't hit. Marvelous Marvin Hagler, still at ringside when Ray made his announcement, said simply, 'It's the story of my life'.

Ray Leonard went back to normal life, or at least what was normal for him. Juanita was due to deliver their second child on or about 22 June, and so Ray went without qualms to Las Vegas to do TV commentary on the 15 June Thomas Hearns–Roberto Duran fight. Then, the night before the fight, Juanita called him at 3 am to say she was on her way to the hospital. Ray rented a Learjet and set off for Washington, then drove to the hospital in the pouring rain in order to be present at the baby's birth. But despite the doctor's efforts to delay the delivery, by the time Ray arrived so had young Jarrel.

With Jarrel, Ray felt the instincts of fatherhood for the first time. When Little Ray had been born out of wedlock, he had been seventeen and not ready to be a father. Moreover, he'd felt deeply guilty about not being able to provide for Juanita and the baby. This time he planned to be there for Jarrel as he had not been for Little Ray.

Juanita had plenty for him to do around the house as well, for she refused to have household help – not a housekeeper or a live-in babysitter. Ray obliged. He was also trying to come up with a plan for a family business that he and Juanita could one day leave to their children. He retained his ties to boxing by continuing as a ringside commentator for HBO. He also got involved with the training of younger fighters. Mike Trainer, who felt that he now had time to pursue his own interests, rather than simply those of Ray Leonard, got into the fight management business that year, representing Shawn O'Sullivan, a Canadian Olympic medallist. At first, Ray simply stopped by the gym to watch O'Sullivan spar, but as time went on he became increasingly involved in the fighter's development, acting as an unpaid cornerman and even sparring with him. To spar with O'Sullivan, Ray found that he had to do more than run daily and go to the health spa; he had to work out more energetically to be in ring shape. Trainer encouraged Ray's involvement with O'Sullivan, thinking that it would get out of his system the itch to get back into the ring.

10

Leonard Meets Hagler at Last

SLIGHTLY LESS THAN two years after his second retirement from professional boxing, Ray Leonard began hinting that he might be persuaded to make yet another comeback. The deciding factor would be whether Marvin Hagler agreed to a title fight. Try as he might, Ray had never been able to get Hagler out of his mind. Hagler was the one fighter Ray considered to be in his class, and deep down he resented the fact that he had never fought him. Each time he did ringside commentary on a Hagler fight for HBO, such as the 15 April 1985 bout in which Hagler knocked Thomas Hearns senseless, he found himself fantasizing that he was in the ring with the middleweight champion and avoiding the mistakes of his hapless opponents. 'I can whip the sucker,' he would tell HBO colleagues. Those close to him noticed that every time he watched a Hagler fight, he would be edgy for a while, he would run more and work out more for a while, before the fire subsided and he went back to his usual routine of keeping in shape. In November, Hagler beat Roberto Duran. Ray did ringside commentary for HBO as usual. After the fight, Duran shouted down to him, 'Leonard, you knock him out, no problem.' After this fight, the fire in Ray did not subside.

That autumn, Mike Trainer and some partners opened a restaurant in Bethesda, Maryland, called Jameson's. Ray, although not an investor in the restaurant, had agreed to lend his presence and his name to the venture, and he invited Marvin Hagler as his first guest. They talked that night about what would have happened had they ever met in the ring, and although they did not reach a consensus on who would have emerged the victor, they did agree that it would have been the fight of the century.

A few months later, on 10 March 1986, Ray did commentary for HBO on a Hagler title defence against John (The Beast) Mugabi. Hagler successfully defended his title with an eleventh round knockout of Mugabi, and the fight fired up Ray Leonard more than usual. Once again, he started working out more, but this time the more energetic regimen did not subside. Ray now began regular sparring matches with Shawn O'Sullivan, the Canadian welterweight with an 11-0 record who was one of the fighters he was managing. Ray was thirty years old now, and his natural weight was about 162 pounds before a match. He felt he could meet Hagler at that weight. He started hinting about a comeback to Juanita. 'I don't want to discuss it,' was all she would say.

On 1 May Ray started talking publicly about coming out of retirment to fight Hagler. It wasn't planned. He was at a Washington fund-raiser when a reporter spotted him and asked if he would ever return to the ring. Yes, said Ray, but only to fight Hagler. Once he said that, he was committed. 'I've always wanted Hagler, I need this man,' he told reporters a few days later. Besides, Ray reasoned, boxing needed a Leonard–Hagler fight to get itself out of the doldrums it had been in recently. Hagler was the only top attraction in boxing who was active at the time, Ray and heavyweight Gerry Cooney having been virtually inactive for the last four years. Ray felt that the game needed a shot in the arm.

Everyone around Ray was against the idea. When questioned by sports writers, Mike Trainer, Ray's attorney, said that Ray's advisers were trying 'to put out the fire'. They saw no sense in his risking his health and his reputation with another fight. He was ring-rusty, he'd had the problems with his eyes. He certainly did not need the money. Trainer estimated that Ray was worth about $20 million, and he had yet to spend a penny of the principal he had earned fighting.

At the time Ray issued his challenge, Marvin Hagler was on a Caribbean cruise and there was no way to reach him. On his return to his home in Brockton, Massachusetts, when asked about Ray Leonard's talk, Hagler just shrugged his shoulders and said, 'I'm not jumping through hoops.' He'd already been twice denied the chance to meet Leonard in the ring. Boxing *aficionados* and sports writers were sceptical as well. There were procedures, after all, and few people felt that Sugar Ray should have a chance at Hagler without first proving himself against ranked contenders. They pointed out that a Leonard–Hagler fight wasn't just up to Hagler but up to the boxing establishment.

Except for the bout against Howard in May 1984, Leonard had not had a fight in four years. Now he wanted boxing authorities to sanction him as a legitimate contender for the middleweight title without even a warm-up bout.

Many compared Leonard with Gerry Cooney, the heavyweight boxer who had also been essentially inactive for four years when he announced that he wanted to challenge Michael Spinks for the heavyweight title. The International Boxing Federation had required him to fight against a ranked contender before meeting Spinks. And some recalled the time when Muhammad Ali had come out of retirement in 1970 to challenge Joe Frazier. First, he had been made to prove himself against Jerry Quarry and Oscar Bonavena before winning the chance to contest with Frazier the following year. It wasn't fair to the boxers who had remained active and paid their dues by fighting up the ladder to a title bout for Ray Leonard or anyone else to expect to be granted a title bout based on a long-ago record. As one sports writer put it, Sugar Ray should have to prove 'he's not Sucaryl Ray by jumping through the hoop of at least one ranked contender'.

Meanwhile, Marvelous Marvin Hagler stayed virtually incommunicado. His manager, Pat Petronelli, had called Trainer to say that Hagler was sure to take the fight, but Hagler would not even talk about it with Petronelli. Two months after Ray's challenge, Hagler, who had admitted to being thirty-two but who was more likely thirty-five, called a press conference in Brockton and announced with considerable emotion that he was thinking of retiring from boxing. He would not, however, rule out entirely a match against Sugar Ray Leonard.

Then, on 18 August, Rich Rose, a spokesman for Top Rank, Bob Arum's promotion company, announced that Hagler would fight Leonard, that Marvelous Marvin did not want to go down in history as the man who ducked Sugar Ray Leonard. The bout would take place the following March, for a $10 million guarantee for Hagler and $5 million for Leonard, and that Top Rank would promote the fight. No word came personally from Hagler, and that bothered Mike Trainer, who suspected that Pat Petronelli had gone off on his own and made a deal with Top Rank, and who did not like Bob Arum and had vowed never again to work with him. There had been no consultation with Trainer or anyone else representing Ray, and the announcement of terms by Top Rank left little room for Trainer to negotiate. Two days later he met Petronelli and warned, 'I hope you haven't done anything that truly prevents this event from happening.'

Meanwhile, Sugar Ray Leonard behaved as if the fight would come off. He religiously did roadwork, hit the bags, and skipped rope every day at the Sugar Ray Leonard Boxing Center in Palmer Park, Maryland. He studied films of Hagler's fights, noting where the champion's opponents had made mistakes, like trying to go toe-to-toe with him. He pooh-poohed speculation that he was too rusty. 'They didn't have what I had,' he said of his critics to a writer for *Sports Illustrated*. 'They didn't feel what I felt. I reached a pinnacle that few men can claim – psychologically, emotionally, spiritually. I want to pick it up where I left it off. I've got to do what I've got to do.'

Mike Trainer was more sceptical. 'Ray Leonard is the kind of guy who's always looking at the edge of the cliff, fascinated as to how close he can get to it. He hasn't gotten to the edge yet.'

Over the next few months, Trainer tried without success to persuade the Petronelli brothers to do the fight without Arum hiring others to put on the bout which would mean more money for the fighters. Realizing that the Hagler camp was set on Arum, Trainer concentrated on getting the best deal he could for Ray. He never negotiated directly with Arum because of their mutual enmity; intermediaries kept Arum apprised of developments and sought his opinion. In the end, Trainer was fairly satisfied with the package he managed to get. Financially, it was much better than the original offer. In addition to an $11 million guarantee, Ray would have the closed-circuit television rights for northern Virginia, Washington, DC, and Maryland. Trainer chose the upfront guarantee rather than a percentage; he wanted Ray to concentrate on the fight, not on the size of the audience.

As important to Ray as, if not more important than, the money, was the fact that Hagler's people had agreed to the fighters wearing thumbless gloves. Another thing that Ray believed would be in his favour was that the fight would take place under the auspices of the WBC, under whose rules title fights were twelve rounds, not fifteen. Of course, Hagler thought that might work in his favour, given that Leonard would be rusty and might take a few rounds to warm up. Negotiations having been concluded, the date and place of the fight were announced: 6 April 1987, at Caesar's Palace in Las Vegas, Nevada.

What about boxing procedures? Why didn't Sugar Ray have to prove himself by fighting a couple of ranked contenders first? But in boxing, dues-paying did not stack up too well against stampeding dollars. It was hardly the first time, and would not be the last, that money and publicity took precedence over 'the way it's s'posed to be'. Boxing purists grumbled, but when tickets for the 15,336 seats in the Caesar's Palace outdoor arena went on sale in November, they were snapped up in a record sixteen days. For Marvelous Marvin Hagler, too, the time had come to forget about the rules and make the money. He had refused any further title defences until after his bout with Leonard, which he had indeed agreed to as of July. In the autumn of 1986, the WBA stripped Hagler of his title, citing the fact that he had not defended it in six months, since the bout with Mugabi on 10 March. By the following April, the IBF was considering a similar action. Hagler didn't much care.

It was billed as 'The SuperFight', and in November Leonard and Hagler began a publicity tour to promote interest (and profit) in the richest prize-fight in history. As comedian Bob Hope quipped at one point in the tour, 'These guys don't worry about income taxes. They just call the IRS (Internal Revenue Service) and ask "How much do you need?"' On that tour, Ray wasted no time starting psychological warfare against Hagler. Knowing that Hagler cultivated enmity toward opponents to inspire the necessary killer instinct in himself, Ray made a point of saying only nice things about him. Hagler finally quit the tour in mid-December, saying he didn't want to see Leonard's face any more until the night of the fight. He remained essentially incommunicado until April.

For his part, Ray Leonard uncharacteristically isolated himself as he went into intensive training for the bout. Arriving at his training camp in Hilton Head, South Carolina, on 22 January 1987, he restricted his contacts with the press to an hour following his midday workout each Monday. His sparring sessions were closed to outsiders. To mollify reporters, his organization distributed frequent handouts containing quotable quotes from Ray Leonard. But press relations just had to take a backseat this time. Ray Leonard knew he was in for the fight of his life, and he was not going to let outside pressure blow his chances.

To some degree, he was copying Hagler's training-camp style, although Hagler's Palm Springs, Florida, camp was Spartan compared to Leonard's. While Leonard still had lots of friends and family around, Hagler had a skeleton staff, mostly of professionals. Few outsiders were allowed in. Hagler ate alone in his room, took only emergency calls even from his family. When Hagler prepared for a fight, he let nothing interfere with his concentration. Ray Leonard realized he had to do much the same. He had one goal, and that was to beat Hagler. He didn't care if the fight was sanctioned. He didn't even care about the title.

'You can call it the Sugar Ray–Marvin Hagler middleweight crown,' he said. 'I just want the fight.'

Marvelous Marvin Hagler, after all, was no Bill Finch or Kevin Howard. He was a bull, with a head so fierce, according to Rick Reilly of *Sports Illustrated*, 'hair is afraid to grow there.' He'd won 62 pro bouts, lost two and drawn two. He was undefeated in the last ten years and he had held on to the middleweight title since 1980; the WBA's action the previous autumn notwithstanding, he *owned* the title. His favourite slogan, 'Destruction and Destroy', might have been ungrammatical but it worked for him. A left-handed fighter who sometimes switched to the right hand, he never let an opponent count on his having a weak side.

Hagler was called the last of the club fighters. He had paid his dues, and then some. He made $50 for his first pro fight (Leonard made $40,000). He didn't get a shot at a title until his 50th fight. (Leonard got his first shot in his 26th fight.) In 1979, when Hagler had his first shot at the middleweight title, his fight against Vito Antuofermo was the undercard bout for Sugar Ray Leonard's fight for the welterweight title against Wilfredo Benitez. Leonard never fought an undercard bout. That night, Leonard made $1 million, Hagler $40,000. That night, Leonard won. For Hagler, the bout was a draw, although experts, among them Joe Louis, contended that Hagler had been robbed. Sugar Ray Leonard had been robbed just once, and that was in his amateur career. 'That taught me a lesson,' Hagler told a writer for *Sports Illustrated* in March 1987. 'You know what they want, man. They only want blood and knockouts. That's all they want. Either you're going to be the bad guy or the good guy. And I ain't never been the good guy.'

Hagler had spent his childhood years in Newark, New Jersey, but the 1968 riots there had persuaded his mother to move the family to Brockton, Massachusetts, which happened to be the home of Rocky Marciano. By the age of sixteen, Marvin was a school dropout and an unmarried father, but he came under the tutelage of Goody and Pat Petronelli, who owned a gym in Brockton and for whose construction company Marvin worked. He never left them, although some observers contended that he might have got a title fight earlier if he had signed with one of the big-name promoters who had often courted him. He fought the club fights, paid his dues from small checks, and all the while watched a young pretty boy named Sugar Ray Leonard win an Olympic gold medal and then go on to fame and glory, not to mention lucrative television commercials. Ray Leonard had always been given things on a silver platter; Marvin Hagler had had to work hard even from crumbs. The SuperFight was going to be more than a fight, it was going to be a classic matchup between a pug and a pugilist, or between a real fighter and a phoney, depending on point of view.

As the fight approached, Las Vegas odds-makers had Ray down by 3-1, which was better than the original 4-1 odds but which still bothered Ray. He knew that people still believed he would be unable to overcome ring-rust. It didn't seem to occur to them that Hagler himself must be a bit rusty, not having fought since March 1986. Nor did it seem to occur to them that Ray Leonard was above all a smart fighter.

Still, those around him were worried that he was concentrating so much on getting himself ready mentally that he was not paying enough attention to his physical training. He wasn't engaging in all-out sparring matches, he wasn't sparring without headgear. He wasn't working as hard as he should. Mike Trainer arranged to have J.D. Brown, a member of Ray's entourage, go to Hagler's training camp and report on what he was doing. Brown dyed his hair partially grey and donned spectacles for the assignment, and brought back a picture of himself with Hagler to prove that he had actually infiltrated the enemy camp. Trainer hoped that Brown's report would inspire Ray to train harder, but it had little effect. Even Juanita Leonard criticized her husband's regimen. But Ray wouldn't listen.

Eventually, Trainer called Angelo Dundee in Miami and had him come to camp early. Dundee flew in on 28 February, five weeks before the fight instead of the usual two or three. Soon, Ray Leonard was listening. He started training harder, and together they worked out a plan. Ray would use his speed and quick reflexes to dance around and confound Hagler for the first three rounds. By the fourth round, tired of chasing Ray, Hagler would go after him more aggressively and get careless. Ray would then connect with some great combination. He would win round after round and would in the end beat Hagler on points.

Two weeks before the SuperFight, the odds against Ray were down to two and a half to one. Excitement was building. Leonard and Hagler underwent 'routine' examination and licensing procedures, which, given Ray Leonard's medical history, were not so routine where he was concerned. Since 1983 there had existed a medical advisory board to advise the Nevada State Athletic Commission on medical safety for fighters, but the head of the board, Dr Charles Filippini, complained that the board had been kept in the dark about the condition of Leonard's eyes. A spokesman for the commission insisted that there was no intention to slight the board, remarking that the board was 'relatively new', but that excuse sounded lame even to the gullible. The real reason was that nobody wanted anything to interfere with the SuperFight. The press picked up the story, and within two days the Nevada State Athletic Commission had ordered Ray to undergo an extensive, two-hour examination by a Las Vegas retinal specialist. He cleared Ray to fight. But Ray's eyes continued to be a major issue for everyone but Ray himself. Hagler didn't help by saying, more than once, 'If he's foolish enough to step in the ring with me, I'm foolish enough to rip his eye out.'

Both camps jockeyed for whatever advantage they could get as fight time approached. When the names of three judges were proposed, Pat Petronelli requested the removal of one, which was his right. He had no quarrel with Dave Moretti or Lou Fillippo, but Harry Gibbs was a British official, and Petronelli, believing that the British preferred straight-up, classic boxers, felt Gibbs would be harder on a rough, tough, swarming boxer like Hagler. In place of Gibbs, Petronelli asked for a judge who would not hold Hagler's fighting style against him. He did not, he said later, ask specifically for a Mexican judge, although that's the way Duane Ford, the chairman of the Nevada State Athletic Commission, remembered it. The Leonard camp had no problem with the change. Meanwhile, the SuperFight was shaping up to be one of the gaudiest shows ever put on in the capital of gaudiness. More than one thousand sports writers had been accredited, including press representatives from thirty-two foreign countries. Hollywood stars, celebrities from television, music and sports had tickets. Thousands more lesser lights had descended on Las Vegas with no hope of getting tickets but just to say they had been there. Between ticket sales and closed-circuit television sales, the fight was expected to gross $70 million, $25 million more than the Larry Holmes–Gerry Cooney fight of four years earlier.

On 3 April, Leonard and Hagler participated in a final pre-fight press conference. Reporters were surprised that the two seemed to have switched personalities for the occasion. Ray, who was usually so comfortable with reporters, seemed ill at ease. He answered questions curtly. Hagler wore a red French Foreign Legion-type cap with earflaps and preened for photographers, asking, 'Do I look OK?' Asked how he wanted to be remembered, he quipped, 'As a guy with long hair, who beat Leonard.' He even smiled when Angelo Dundee needled him about his age, saying he was 'a man of all ages'. He predicted that he would knock out Leonard. Ray, on the other hand, declined to make a prediction about the fight's outcome.

Ray was nervous, yes, but it was a positive nervousness, the kind that got the adrenalin flowing. He was uncharacteristically uncommunicative at the press conference because he didn't want to break his concentration. He had developed a vision of Hagler that was constantly with him, the first image he saw when he awoke in the morning. He didn't want to mess with his obsession.

He was ready. For more than a month he and Angelo Dundee had studied films of Hagler's fights and discussed strategy against him. In sparring matches, Ray's partners had acted out assigned roles designed to rehearse him for what might happen in the ring against Hagler. They noticed that when Hagler threw a double jab, he would slide to the right, so Ray practised sliding to his right so that he wouldn't be there to take the jabs. Dundee advised Ray that Hagler was a sucker for a right-hand counter, so Ray practised that. They both noticed that Hagler tended to flatten out in the middle rounds, so their plan was for Ray to win the early rounds and then take a couple in the middle, forcing Hagler to try to make up for lost points when he was least able to. It all sounded good. The question was: would it work?

On the morning of Monday, 6 April 1987, Leonard and Hagler met at the Sports Pavilion, an indoor facility at Caesar's Palace, for the weigh-in. Ray entered first, to some cheering and applause, but hardly a roar of welcome. There was clearly some feeling that he didn't really deserve to be taking on the middleweight champion. When Hagler arrived a few minutes later, he got the roar of approval from the crowd. Ray weighed in at 158 pounds, 2 ounces, Hagler at 158 pounds, 8 ounces. Hagler stared at his opponent, but Ray refused to make eye contact. Little Ray, however, who was present at the weigh-in, did enough staring for the Leonard family; his eyes widened as he looked Hagler up and down.

On Monday night, 6 April 1987, Sugar Ray Leonard and Marvelous Marvin Hagler met in the promised SuperFight. Again, it was clear that Hagler was the favourite, but Ray refused to let that bother him. He danced around the Pointer Sisters as they sang the national anthem. There was a huge fireworks display. Then the two fighters perfunctorily touched gloves without making eye contact. Ray now weighed 163 pounds, having studiously added weight for stamina. The bell rang for the start of Round 1, and Ray came out dancing. He circled the ring, Hagler in pursuit. They talked to one another. Later, Leonard said that Hagler called him a sissy. For his part, Leonard made faces, taunting his opponent in much the same way as he had done to Roberto Duran. Neither man landed any damaging punches.

In the second round, Leonard scored points with several single punches, but no combinations. He was too busy getting out of Hagler's reach to land more than one punch. His tactic was to 'stick and dip', as Angelo Dundee kept yelling from Ray's corner. When he didn't dip, he clutched Hagler until referee Richard Steele moved in to break it up.

Hagler, who was getting frustrated, landed his first good punch, a left to the head, early in Round 3. But Ray fought back, finally connecting with a left-right combination later in the round. In turn, Hagler connected with a right to the head as the bell rang. But Ray kept up the psychological pressure, ignoring closing bells and coming out of his corner before the rounds even began.

Ray continued to make faces at Hagler, and to score, in the fourth round. Each time he landed a punch, he would either spin away or tie Hagler up. At one point, Hagler nailed him with a left as he tried to tie him up. The two exchanged verbal insults. At another point, Ray wound up a right-hand bolo, but instead of a left jab, which he had delivered to Roberto Duran, he caught Hagler with a right to the stomach.

By the fifth round Hagler had decided he'd had enough of this butterfly. He pressured Ray, hammering him with short blows at close range. Boxed in, Ray had no choice but to stand and fight, especially when Hagler cornered him against the ropes. But Ray was up to the challenge. While against the ropes, he landed a couple of sharp combinations. He refused to be bullied, and he proved to Hagler that he could take his punches, although a couple of them hurt him. He also made a mental note that Hagler was not landing any combinations, just single punches.

Ray was tired in the sixth round, and fought flat-footed, shoring up his strength for the coming rounds. Still, he managed to get through the round without being hit hard. In Rounds 7 and 8 Hagler scored more points. Ray realized that, ironically, it was he, not Hagler, who was going flat in the middle rounds.

In the ninth round, Ray was so tired that his legs were beginning to wobble, and on two different occasions, it appeared that Hagler had him in trouble in a corner. But Ray flurried away out of trouble. Just seconds after one such potential disaster, at mid-ring, Ray caught Hagler with a right-left combination. The crowd roared its approval. The mood was changing, and now there was a new respect for the skill of Sugar Ray, but especially for his tenacity, his courage, his 'heart'. Aware that the crowd was turning his way, Ray regained his steam and in the last two rounds especially danced around as nimbly as he had in the first few. He also landed more punches than Hagler did.

In the corner, Angelo Dundee was all smiles. 'One more round, Champ,' he said after the eleventh. Ray smiled, too, and stood to give the crowd a raised glove. Hagler did the same, indicating, although he didn't mean to, just who was in control. Back out in the ring Ray gave Hagler another taunting smile. By his own count, the only way Hagler could win was by a knockout, and Ray didn't intend to cooperate. The crowd chanted 'Sugar Ray, Sugar Ray,' and Ray danced to the rhythm. Two minutes into the round, he glanced back at Dundee with the question, how much more time. Dundee yelled one minute, and Ray, who had shed 13 pounds in the course of the fight, danced around out of reach for the remaining 60 seconds.

When the final bell rang, Ray raised his hands above his head in victory and then looked over at the judges, who were busily comparing score cards. Moments later, ring announcer Chuck Hull declared it was a split decision and that Sugar Ray Leonard had won. Spontaneously, Ray grabbed the microphone and shouted, 'Thank you, thank you. I will see you in six months and 15 pounds later.' The obvious implication of that statement was that he planned to go on fighting, but he later demurred, saying he was only kidding.

In the pandemonium that followed, it was hard to hear what was said in the ring. Some people thought they heard Hagler mutter, 'Sugar Ray Leonard, of all people.' Hagler was certain he heard Leonard say to him, 'You beat me, man.' But Ray insists he never said that, that he was certain all along that he had won. What he did say to Hagler was, 'You're still the champ,' for the title had never been what he was after in a fight with Marvin Hagler.

Here is how the judges had scored the fight: Dave Moretti of Las Vegas had Ray ahead 115-113 (seven rounds to five). Lou Fillippo of Los Angeles had Hagler ahead 115-113 (also seven rounds to five). But Jo Jo Guerra of Monterrey, Mexico, had Leonard ahead 118-110, having given Hagler only two rounds of the twelve, the fifth and the twelfth. Few experts agreed with that lopsided scoring, although some had scored the fight nine rounds for Leonard and three for Hagler. Among reporters, some had one or the other fighter far ahead, some had one or the other slightly ahead, and still others had scored the fight a draw. But the decision of the three judges stood.

The scoring of boxing matches is complicated, and no one denies that the 'human element' plays a part. Once, a computer title match was arranged between Muhammad Ali and Rocky Marciano. Computer programmers in England and in the United States inputted the information. In England, Ali won, while in the United States Marciano won, proving that the 'human element' is present even in what ought to have been the most objectively scored dream fight in history.

Evaluating a boxer for artistry, effectiveness of punches, and control of the fight, judges score each round by points. On analysis, Guerra's scoring turned out to be not all that different from that of his fellows. He had agreed with one or the other of them in nine out of twelve rounds, and in the three rounds in which he had disagreed, the other two judges had scored them very close, ten points to nine. The other two judges had disagreed with each other in four of the twelve rounds.

An analysis of the fight seemed to back up the decision. Hagler had thrown a total of 792 punches, and missed on 502. Leonard had thrown 629 and missed 323. Hagler connected on 291, Leonard on 306. Hagler's partisans charged that Leonard's punches were 'powder puffs'. Leonard's countered that boxing was supposed to be the sweet science, as essayist A. J. Liebling had put it, not a barroom brawl, and that Sugar Ray had been the matador to

Hagler's bull.

In Hagler's opinion, he'd been robbed again. This time, he thought it was because the boxing establishment did not want him to retire, which he had threatened to do the previous year. Either that, or they wanted to set up a return match. But the judge who had given Ray the fight by a slight edge pointed out that you couldn't chase and get hit and get credit for it. At no point had Hagler effectively gone after his opponent. In retrospect, Petronelli said he wished he had told his fighter to go out and get Leonard in the first few rounds.

It took Ray Leonard several days to realize that the fight had actually happened and that he'd won. The fight, not to mention the months of preparation, had been so physically and emotionally draining that he was disoriented. He didn't even feel victorious. But gradually he began to be aware of just what he had done. He had disproved conventional fighting wisdom that a boxer can't come back. He had won against the odds. He had become the tenth fighter in history to win three different world titles. And, what's more, he had come back to beat Marvelous Marvin Hagler without even a tune-up. He realized that Angelo Dundee and his strategy had had a great deal to do with the win, but he also knew that he had been smart enough to listen to Dundee, unlike Muhammad Ali. And he had been the one who, at the age of thirty, was still in shape enough to dance around Marvin Hagler for most of twelve rounds and to withstand all the blows that Hagler had dealt him.

Ray Leonard understood Hagler's feeling. That championship belt had been the centre of Hagler's life. Said Ray later, 'As much as I wanted to beat him, I wish there was a way I could have beaten him and could have said, "Here's your belt."'

Ray did not want either boxing or a championship belt to be the centre of his life. He decided against continuing. He had done what he set out to do. He was satisfied, content with himself, at peace. He had nothing more to prove. In May, he announced his fourth official retirement (his third from the pro game). Those who loved him breathed a sigh of relief. He had everything to gain by staying retired this time.

Once again, Ray went back to 'civilian' life. In July, because of his great admiration of Eddie Robinson, football coach at the all-black Grambling University, he established the Sugar Ray Leonard Scholarship Fund with a grant of $250,000. In August, he signed a one-year contract with the Mutual Broadcasting System to host a radio talk show interviewing fellow athletes. In September, he announced that he had entered into an agreement with Madison Square Garden to promote his new boxing team, which he had not yet formed. Meanwhile, he continued to do sports commentary for HBO, watching from a vantage point that few others enjoyed as twenty-year-old heavyweight Mike Tyson dashed thirty-eight-year-old Larry Holmes' comeback hopes in January 1988.

11

Triumph of a 'Little Old Man'

ON THE OTHER hand, the Tyson-Holmes fight might just have been the spur to Sugar Ray's itch to come out of retirement yet again. He was now thirty-one years old, ordinarily a fighter's prime, but the clock was ticking away. If he ever wanted to fight again, he would have to do so soon. He couldn't wait until he was thirty-eight, as Larry Holmes had.

He was restless for the ring. It was the one place where, as a child, he got the respect that meant so much to him, and that feeling of being most whole when he was in the ring had never left him. But Sugar Ray Leonard had never entered a ring just for the hell of it. Each time, he had been in pursuit of a goal, and now another goal loomed for him.

Back in October, Thomas Hearns had knocked out Juan Roldan for the WBC middleweight title, becoming the first boxer in history to win four world crowns. That had set Ray to thinking that he had won only three such championships, and that he was merely one of ten to have achieved that distinction. It was rumoured that the WBC was considering the creation of a new weight class, the super middleweight (168 pound limit). Ray wanted to win a fourth boxing title, as Thomas Hearns had done, and the logical one was the new title. Moreover, if he could challenge the WBC light heavyweight champion, Donny Lalonde, and persuade the WBC to let them fight simultaneously for both the super middleweight and light heavyweight crowns, then he would have a shot at becoming the first boxer in history to win championships in *five* weight classes. Now that was a goal he couldn't resist.

By the end of March the rumours were flying fast and thick that Sugar Ray Leonard would make yet another comeback. Mike Trainer had requested films of WBC light heavyweight champion Donny Lalonde's fights. He had also cancelled several promotional appearances scheduled for Ray later in the year. There were reports that Jose Sulaiman, president of the WBC, had been approached about a simultaneous title fight and was interested in the idea.

Naturally, there was criticism in the fight world over Ray's seemingly singular ability to come out of retirement at whim to fight in title matches that other fighters had to work years to get. But Ray answered his critics by pointing out that there was a stipulation in pro boxing rules that a champion who had exemplified greatness was given the right to choose title matches. 'It's all out of respect,' he said, 'like when Ali came back, and Joe Louis and Larry Holmes, right down the line.' [L. King]

With the rumours came offers for Ray to fight other boxers, but he wasn't interested in mere fights. He wanted a double-title fight against Lalonde or nothing, and not until the end of July, when he was fairly certain that Lalonde and the WBC would go along with the idea, did Ray Leonard announce officially that he was coming out of retirement yet again.

In this, he had the full backing of his wife, Juanita, because he had promised her that this time he would stay *un*-retired. According to Ray, 'My wife was the one to say, "Ray, either keep fighting or don't retire anymore, you just can't continue to do that." I, in fact, got tired of myself retiring and unretiring, and that won't be the case any more.' [L. King]

Meanwhile, Leonard's and Lalonde's people were shopping around for sites. Reportedly, they wanted $5 to $6 million for live-site rights, and both Caesar's Palace and the Golden Nugget were among the bidders willing to pay that amount. Also in the running were a Japanese group and a city in China.

On 3 August, Leonard and Lalonde signed a contract for a twelve-round bout for the two WBC titles simultaneously. No date had been set, but the bout was slated for October or November. By the terms of the contract, Lalonde, whose normal weight was 175 pounds, agreed to weigh no more than 168 pounds. Leonard, who weighed 156 pounds that day, said he expected to weigh 161–162 by fight time. Under the contract there were no monetary guarantees; both fighters would take percentages. However, based on site fees, ticket sales, and anticipated closed-circuit TV revenues, Lalonde stood to make at least $5 million and Leonard at least $12 million. Moreover, the bout finances were structured so that the fighters were partners in a venture that allowed them to split the lion's share of the profits, and made those who actually staged the bout in essence hired hands. The promoters for this fight would be Victory Promotions and Caesar's Palace. Titan Promotions would handle the distribution of pay-per-view TV, which was usually their market.

Donny Lalonde was a different kind of opponent for Ray. One big difference was that he was white. A twenty-eight-year-old, dyed-blond, handsome Canadian whose nickname was 'Golden Boy', he was a vegetarian who took acting classes and had even performed in a two-character off-off Broadway play called *Just Keep Listening*. He liked to read about Zen Buddhism. He claimed to have taught the Edmonton Oilers hockey star Wayne Gretzky how to skate. He had taught himself the real estate business and made money at it; he shuttled among homes in Winnipeg, Manitoba, New Haven, Connecticut, and Greenwich Village in New York City. His fight record left something to be desired, his two most recent victories having been over Trinidadian Leslie Stewart who was both older and more tired. Some critics said that Ray should have tried to fight Ivan Barkley or Michael Nunn, although both were under contract to Bob Arum and so anathema to the Leonard camp. They were missing the point. Only with Lalonde were two titles at stake. And it was the two titles that Ray was after.

The news electrified Thomas Hearns. He'd been knocked

out by Barkley in June and had announced *his* retirement. But once he heard that Ray Leonard was after a simultaneous fourth and fifth title, he decided he wanted to win a fifth title, and *before* Leonard could have a chance to win his. Bob Arum quickly got to work, and soon announced that Hearns would meet Thomas Kinchen for the WBA super middleweight title in Las Vegas on either 28 October or 4 November.

On 19 August, at a press conference in Manhattan, Ray and Lalonde confirmed 7 November as the date and Las Vegas as the site for their bout. Inevitably, Ray was asked why he was coming out of retirement, and for the hundredth time he answered that question, this time saying simply, 'I enjoy it. I enjoy the challenge.' [*NYT* 8. 19. 88]

Whether Lalonde was going to be a sufficient challenge for him was doubtful to some people. There was no question that Lalonde had 'heart'. He'd come up the hard way, learning to fight to protect himself in the tough low-income housing development in Vancouver, BC, where he grew up. But while he was able to defend himself against his peers, he was no match for his stepfather, who beat both him and his mother regularly between the years when Lalonde was eleven and fifteen. At the age of fifteen Lalonde hit back for the first time ever, and woke up on the floor. The very next day, he and a friend hitch-hiked 1,300 miles to Kitchener, where his natural father and sister lived.

He was seventeen when he watched an amateur fight on television and decided to become a boxer. Self-trained by sparring with his brother, he had an undistinguished amateur career before turning pro. By early in his pro career he had suffered a shoulder injury in a hockey game that would require surgery twice and that would inhibit the range of motion of his left arm. He compensated by developing a quick and powerful right jab. In the fifth fight of his pro career, he suffered his first loss, and afterwards parted ways with his manager and trainer, buying out his contract. He then tried managing himself and occasionally even promoting his own fights. There were nights when he didn't make a dime in either his capacity as promoter or as fighter. After suffering his second pro loss, Lalonde realized he needed the help of a manager and trainer so he could concentrate on training rather than on business.

In the summer of 1985, when he was twenty-five, he moved to New York, where he found Teddy Atlas to train him and Dave Wolf, a former journalist, to manage him. Fighting in out-of-the-way cities like Enid, Oklahoma, and Mentor, Ohio, Lalonde scored eight straight knockouts in 1986. However, he had injured the middle knuckle of his right hand. By April 1987 his left elbow was in a brace and he had knee problems. Fortunately, he met Ken Balson, who specialized in deep muscle massage and whose treatment relieved much of Lalonde's pain. After an absence of seven months, he returned to the ring under a new trainer, Tommy Gallagher, and defeated Mustafa Hamsho by decision in May 1987 and in November of the same year knocked out Eddie Davies in two rounds to win the WBC light heavyweight title.

Thus, Lalonde was a courageous underdog with a lot against him. Ray Leonard, by contrast, had had a relatively smooth career, marred only by the eye injury. As the fight approached, odds-makers favoured Leonard by 3-1. But Lalonde was confident, calling Leonard a 'little old man', who'd 'had his day'.

There was comparatively little pre-fight psyching. Both men acted more like business partners than boxing opponents. They appeared together in a beer commercial and travelled together on a private jet for a publicity tour. But the attempt to gain a psychological edge was irresistible. The Leonard camp, complaining that Lalonde and his people raced to be first on the jet, took to booking commercial flights instead. Lalonde and his people complained that Leonard flaunted his wealth every chance he got. Eventually, both pulled back from actively publicizing the event and as fight night approached, concentrated on serious training. Ray trained at his camp in Scotron, Pennsylvania. His routine was much the same as in previous years and for earlier fights. But there was one major difference this time: Angelo Dundee was nowhere to be found. For the first time since he had turned pro, Ray Leonard would not have the advice and help of his renowned cornerman.

After Ray's win over Marvelous Marvin Hagler in early 1987, Mike Trainer had praised Dundee to the skies, asserting that Dundee 'probably had as much and maybe more to do with Ray winning than anybody'. [NYT 11. 6. 88] But the trainer's cheque that Dundee had later received had not reflected that contribution. While $175,000 was nothing to sneeze at, it was a tiny fraction of the $12 million that Leonard had won. Moreover, it was an unpleasant surprise, since Dundee, without a contract specifying a percentage, had no way of knowing what he would be paid.

The usually easygoing Dundee was angry, and he let Leonard and Trainer know that he wanted a contract for the Lalonde fight. While waiting to hear their response, he set to work studying tapes of Lalonde's fights and figuring out strategy for Ray. 'I had it all written down,' he told reporters. 'What my guy should do. What my guy shouldn't do. But then I found out he's not my guy any more. After ten years, all I wanted was a contract instead of having to wait until after the fight to find out how much I got. Ten years of this, all I wanted was a contract'. [NYT 11. 6. 88]

It was highly unusual for Dundee to say so much in public, for traditionally he was close-mouthed about his business transactions. The fact that he did allow his bitterness to show indicates the extent of his hurt. But Ray Leonard insisted that he was hurt, too, that he'd had to learn from a reporter that Dundee was not going to assist in his training. 'Angelo never showed any type of dissatisfaction over what I had paid him', said Leonard. 'All of this (problem) was done through third parties. I felt that it was a personal matter between Angelo Dundee and myself. I made numerous attempts to call Angelo, but then the fight was made and I could not deviate from my concentration.' [L. King] Ray would miss Dundee, but he did not believe he needed Dundee to beat Lalonde. He intended to prove that he could beat

Lalonde without Dundee, with only Janks Morton and Dave Jacobs in his corner.

Still, the Dundee story was bad press for Ray, who was not accustomed to bad press. The general sentiment was that Ray had forsaken a friend and supporter who had seen him through many a tough fight, that money meant more to him than loyalty and friendship.

Both Leonard and Lalonde packed up with their respective camps and went out to Las Vegas a few days before the bout. Both ceased intensive training and had more time for the press. There was some animosity between them, but refreshingly the subject of race never came up. Nor was the fact that Lalonde was white and Leonard black exploited by the press. No doubt it was a difference that loomed large in the minds of some fight *aficionados,* but they were not the type of people whose thoughts were given a public hearing. One suspects that it might have been different had Hagler, for example, been Lalonde's opponent, but Sugar Ray Leonard was so squeaky-clean, so different, that race had never plagued him as it had some of his peers.

What the press continued to harp on, where Leonard was concerned, was why the thirty-two-year-old fighter would risk his health and his champion status to climb back into the ring again. His insistence that it was the challenge was given short shrift. More space was devoted to quotes from unidentified sources suggesting that he had become intoxicated by his success against Marvin Hagler or that he simply did not know when to take leave of his brutal profession. And where Lalonde was concerned, there were the continual reminders that despite a pro record of 31–2, with 26 knockouts, despite his numerous injuries, the twenty-eight-year-old had never faced such a high-pressure bout.

On Friday, 4 November, at the Las Vegas Hilton, Thomas Hearns became the first champion of the newly created World Boxing Association's first world title, its super middleweight crown, in a decision over Thomas Kinchen. He also became the first boxer in history to win five world titles, beating Leonard to the punch, so to speak. Leonard refused to let that bother him. Leonard called that fight a preliminary to his bout with Lalonde, but Hearns refused to be angry. He announced that come Monday night he was going to be Leonard's biggest fan, for he wanted Ray to beat Lalonde; he wanted to meet Ray Leonard in the ring again and avenge his loss of seven years earlier.

At the final news conference the day before the fight, Lalonde exuded confidence, reminding his listeners of the size differential between them and saying that he would be fighting 'an old welterweight'. Ray's tongue-in-cheek reaction was, 'He's right. I'm slow and I'm old. I'll be very cautious, and hope he gets tired.' But Ray had earlier given reporters his impersonation of Lalonde as heavy-footed and mechanical, like Frankenstein's monster.

At the official weigh-in the following morning, Lalonde was true to his word and tipped the scales at 167. Ray weighed 165, which was his heaviest weight ever; only after the fight did he admit, 'This morning I didn't weigh any 165. I had things in my pocket.' He felt he needed the psychological advantage that the appearance of a few extra pounds would provide. By this time, the odds were down to 2½-1 in his favour; odds-makers had clearly been affected by all the talk of his age and ring rust, not to mention the height differential (6 ft 1¾ in vs. 5 ft 10½ in) and that of the reach (77 in vs. 74 in). Ray refused to shake hands with Lalonde at the weigh-in. In response, Lalonde stepped to the microphone and said, 'I knew I was fighting an old welterweight; now I know I'm fighting a *fat* old welterweight.'

The weather that evening was mild and breezy, but still by fight time the teperature inside Caesar's Palace arena was 75 degrees. Leonard entered the ring first, wearing a black sequinned robe with gold braid along the shoulders. Lalonde followed in the same colours, black velvet with gold trim. Leonard moved around the ring before the start of the bout, repeatedly brushing past Lalonde. More psyching. This time he was psyching himself as much as Lalonde, for about two weeks before the bout he'd had a premonition that Lalonde would knock him down during the fight and he had no liking for that prospect.

The opening bell for the scheduled twelve-round bout rang and the two fighters were cautious, moving around each other, sizing up one another. No serious punches were thrown in the entire first round, but it was clear from the outset that Lalonde intended to use his supposedly disabled left. The teflon pin and the restricted motion notwithstanding, he let loose several lefts, none of which scored. Round 2 began with more of the same, but with lightning quickness Leonard scored with a right jab to the head. Lalonde raised his arms to show that the punch had not bothered him, then continued to punch with his left, scoring a couple of times, though Leonard was usually able to elude him. In most of the third round, Leonard stayed out of range. Lalonde landed a few rights, but they were essentially without impact. Then Ray moved inside, trying to deprive Lalonde of the leverage necessary for his right hook. He tried to clinch Lalonde, who responded by wrestling Ray into the ropes. Referee Richard Steele stepped in to separate the fighters.

As Round 4 began, spectators were beginning to whisper that this was a dull fight and that both boxers, especially Leonard, seemed to be too cautious. Lalonde had been by far the busier fighter. Then suddenly all that changed. Lalonde finally connected with a right to the head and knocked Leonard to the canvas on the seat of his pants. It was only the second time Ray had ever been knocked down in his pro career, the first having been in the fight against Ken Howard in 1984. Stunned, Leonard wondered what had hit him, for he felt no pain, not even dizziness. As Lalonde raised a hand in triumph, Ray was up in a flash to take the mandatory 8-count, relieved in a way that his apprehension over the premonition was now behind him: the premonition had come true and he was none the worse for it. Lalonde exploited his advantage, stalking Leonard and landing a right that opened a small cut on the left side of his nose, right beside the eye on which he'd had surgery. By the time the round ended, the crowd was clearly rooting for the underdog Lalonde.

In Ray's corner, Eddie the 'cut man' applied salve to the

side of his nose. There was no Angelo Dundee there to apply the small metal cut stauncher. Morton and Jacobs tried to give Ray the type of advice that Dundee would have given had he been there: stop being so cautious, go after him. You're blowing it, kid. Ray realized that the big bout had not intimidated Lalonde. He knew he was behind on the three judges' score cards and needed little encouragement; the knockdown had woken him up. As he had done in crucial moments in the past, he reached down into his reservoir of will and stamina and came out strong in Round 5, scoring with combinations of stiff jabs with left and right hooks. He had found his rhythm now, was using more head movement, and was visibly pleased, a slight smile on his lips as the round ended. The crowd responded by cheering his courage. Lalonde, meanwhile, buoyed by the knockdown and the reaction of the crowd, grew a bit careless with his punches, throwing far more than he landed, although he connected with some solid ones. Still, the round was Leonard's. He'd had to come back, and he had.

In the sixth round, Ray began to discover ways to throw Lalonde off his rhythm, moving and scoring several times with left jabs to the head. It was as though he was shaking off the ring rust. Lalonde, realizing the tide was turning against him, got reckless, charging forward to land his punches. He scored once with his right. In the seventh, Leonard continued with his combinations. Lalonde appeared to be tiring and to be throwing careless punches. He connected on only 21 per cent of his punches in that round, while Ray connected on 57 per cent. In the eighth round Lalonde, who had thrown very few combinations, hurt Leonard with a straight right and a right uppercut. Leonard fought back, stepping inside and scoring with another left hook just as the bell ended the round.

By now the crowd was cheering every good punch, enjoying the match which had been so dull at the start. Both fighters were giving their all, and the crowd roared its approval. Ray was fighting nearly all three minutes of every round, not just one minute, as he had against Hagler the year before. Two judges had Ray ahead five rounds to three going into the ninth, the third judge had the rounds even but Lalonde ahead by one point. As the ninth round began, both men were cheered loudly. In response, Lalonde got off a quick right, followed by a right uppercut, both of which clearly hurt Leonard. But Ray answered with a flurry of combinations. He was fighting harder than he had in years, and with uncharacteristic fury, almost brawling with his opponent. But what a fight the bout had turned into! Then, with two minutes gone in the round, Ray threw a flurry of punches ending with a powerful left hook that literally floored his opponent. When Lalonde got to his feet, he was bleeding from a cut over his left eye. Leonard gave him no chance to recover, but knocked him down again with another left hook. This time Lalonde didn't get up. In fact, as soon as he hit the canvas, referee Steele signalled the end of the fight two minutes and thirty seconds into the round.

Later, the two fighters had nothing but good things to say about one another. Lalonde spoke of Ray's durability and his ability to take several good shots to the head, his skill at defending himself when he was hurt. 'I didn't stick to my original game plan,' he said, 'which at the very beginning was to chase him down. I started waiting on him.' Ray was gracious in victory, averring that his opponent was a bigger and stronger man than he had expected. 'If he maintains the same type of intensity and focus he did with me, there's no question Donny will be a champion again.' [NYT 11.9.88] It was easy to be magnanimous, for Ray had met yet another challenge he had set for himself. He had just made history by winning a record five world championship titles in the course of his career. Except for Hearns three days earlier, no one else had done that. And what's more, he had won the two titles that night decisively – by a knockout. It was ruled a technical knockout only because Lalonde was not actually knocked unconscious. However, it had been more than two minutes before he'd been able to get up.

In a short time Ray would have to relinquish one of the two titles he had won that night, for boxing rules do not permit a fighter to hold more than one title at once. More than likely, he would give up the light heavyweight crown, because he was not really a light heavyweight, his normal weight being 160–162. 'Donny Lalonde reassured me that I am not a light heavyweight,' he said. 'Fighting Lalonde was just a challenge. I don't think I give myself a chance to perform by fighting bigger men.' [HBO] Nevertheless, he had claimed them.

What next for Sugar Ray Leonard? He refused even to speculate. 'All I want to do is go home and enjoy my family,' he said, 'spend Thanksgiving and Christmas with my family. Then, after I look at the tape [of the Lalonde bout] I'll see where to go from there.' [NBC]

One thing was certain, he would not announce another retirement. He'd made that promise when he'd come out of his last retirement. He didn't know how much longer he would fight, but he believed he had at least one more major bout in him. He knew that Thomas Hearns was waiting for him. It would take him a while to decide whether giving Hearns satisfaction was also good business for him. Then there was Michael Nunn. While both potential opponents had ties to Bob Arum, in the fight business there were usually ways to bury hatchets when big, big money was at stake. There were others.

For the time being, he was going to enjoy the high of the win, a high that he always found difficult to explain to those who had never been in a ring. 'It's sort of like sky-diving,' he has said. 'The majority of individuals think it's crazy, but for those people that do it, they find it exhilarating, there's a burst of energy that is indescribable.' [L. King]

'People say that thirty-two years old is time to retire,' Ray continued. 'But I don't want to retire, because I'm still physically and mentally capable. I fight because I want to fight, because I *can* fight; it's quite simple.' [NBC]

Perhaps it was time to take Sugar Ray Leonard at his word. He had shown over and over again that he was capable of doing exactly what he said he would. He didn't put much store by deep psychological explanations for his actions, though to outside observers the suspicion continued that beneath the multi, multi-millionaire, smart-businessman exterior lurked a poor little street kid whose lifetime experience of being 'somebody' was linked inextricably to the boxing ring.

Sugar Ray Leonard had it all, but it was not enough. Objective observers still felt he should quit while he was ahead. On the other hand, they believed that Sugar Ray Leonard had been good for boxing, and that as long as he was in the game in the highly visible capacity as contender, his presence could only continue to help the game. In part, he is responsible for a number of talented young men who have entered boxing, inspired by his success and by his personality and character. And in the main, his bouts, and all the promotion and hype surrounding them, have been businesslike and clean, far removed from the smoke-filled rooms and mob connections that have cast such a pall on the sport. He, and his way of doing business, have marked the fight game in the 1980s. In fact, while heavyweight Muhammad Ali dominated the sport in the 1970s, and heavyweight Mike Tyson, if he can get his priorities straight, may well be the fighter of the 1990s, Sugar Ray Leonard, welterweight, junior middleweight, middleweight, super middleweight and light heavyweight, is without question the fighter of the 1980s. Indeed, he may well be remembered as the fighter who saved the game.

SUGAR RAY LEONARD'S PROFESSIONAL CAREER RECORD

Year	Date	Opponent	Decision	
1977	5 February	Luis Vega	W-6 rounds	
	14 May	Willie Rodriguez	W-6	
	10 June	Vinnie DeBarros	KO-3	
	24 September	Frank Santore	KO-5	
	5 November	Augustine Estrada	KO-6	
	17 December	Hector Diaz	KO-2	
1978	4 February	Rocky Ramon	W-8	
	1 March	Art McKnight	KO-7	
	19 March	Javier Muniz	KO-1	
	13 April	Bobby Haymon	KO-3	
	13 May	Randy Milton	KO-8	
	3 June	Rafael Rodriguez	W-10	
	18 July	Dick Ecklund	W-10	
	9 September	Floyd Mayweather	KO-10	
	6 October	Randy Shields	W-10	
	3 November	Bernardo Prada	W-10	
	9 December	Armando Muniz	KO-6	
1979	11 January	Johnny Gant	KO-8	
	11 February	Fernand Marcotte	KO-8	
	24 March	Daniel Gonzales	KO-1	
	21 April	Adolpho Viruet	W-10	
	20 May	Marcos Geraldo	W-10	
	24 June	Tony Chiaverini	KO-4	
	12 August	Pete Ranzany	KO-4	
	28 September	Andy Price	KO-1	
	30 November	Wilfredo Benitez	KO-15	WBC Welterweight title
1980	31 March	Davey Green	KO-4	Title defence
	20 June	Roberto Duran	L-15	Lost WBC title
	25 November	Roberto Duran	KO-8	Regained WBC title
1981	28 March	Larry Bonds	KO-10	
	25 June	Ayub Kalule	TKO-9	WBA Junior Middle-weight title
	16 September	Thomas Hearns	TKO-14	Consolidated WBA and WBC Welter-weight titles
1982	15 February	Bruce Finch	TKO-3	
1983	10 May	Kevin Howard	TKO-9	
1987	6 April	Marvin Hagler	W-12	WBA Middleweight title
1988	7 November	Donny Lalonde	TKO-9	WBC Super Middle-weight and Light-Heavyweight title

Selected Bibliography

Books

Goldstein, Alan. *A Fistful of Sugar: The Sugar Ray Leonard Story*. New York: Coward McCann & Geoghegan, 1981.

Toperoff, Sam. *Sugar Ray Leonard and Other Noble Warriors*. New York: McGraw Hill, 1987.

Magazine Articles

Axhelm, Pete. 'America's Fighter.' *Newsweek,* 10 December 1979, p. 133.

—— 'Sugar's Sweetest Confection.' *Newsweek,* 20 April 1987, p. 71.

Berger, Phil. 'Dundee: Champ of Corner Men.' *The New York Times Magazine,* 29 November 1981, pp. 34–5 *et seq.*

Callahan, Tom. 'Boxing's Allure.' *Time,* 27 June 1988, pp. 66–71.

—— 'Too Moving To Be Mayhem.' *Time,* 20 April 1987, p. 62.

'Eye TKO: Surgery for Sugar Ray.' *Time,* 24 May 1982, p. 85.

Friedman, Jack. 'Can Sugar Ray Leonard Make a Comeback? Don't Even Ask.' *People,* 30 March 1987, pp. 58–60.

Hamill, Pete. 'The Greatest Street Fighter.' *New York,* 23 June 1980, p. 26 *et seq.*

—— 'Those Whispers About Duran.' *New York,* 15 December 1980, pp. 34–6 *et seq.*

Katz, Michael. 'Fists Full of Dollars: Hearns Takes on Leonard.'*The New York Times Magazine,* 13 September 1981, pp. 142–4 *et seq.*

Leonard, Ray Charles, as told to Pat Putnam. 'I Just Don't Want To Fight Anymore.' *Sports Illustrated,* 15 November 1982, pp. 34–6 *et seq.*

'Leonard Rides Wave of Success to Radio Show.' *Jet,* 3 August 1987, p. 49.

Linderman, Lawrence. 'Playboy Interview: Sugar Ray Leonard.'

Playboy, May 1982, pp. 81–2 *et seq.*

Nack, William. 'Angling in on Roberto.' *Sports Illustrated,* 24 November 1980, pp. 43–5 *et seq.*

'The Big Bellyache.' *Sports Illustrated,* 8 December 1980, pp. 26–9.

'Everything I Did Worked.' *Sports Illustrated,* 20 April 1987, pp. 50–3.

'Let the World Know I'm O.K.' *Sports Illustrated,* 28 September 1987, pp. 34–7.

'On Top of the World.' *Sports Illustrated,* 10 December 1979, pp. 27–8 *et seq.*

'Prediction.' *Sports Illustrated,* 30 March 1987, pp. 70–2 *et seq.*

'Right On For Roberto.' *Sports Illustrated,* 30 June 1980, pp. 15–21.

'There is a Burning Desire in Me.' *Sports Illustrated,* 8 September 1986, pp. 28–30 *et seq.*

Norman, Michael. 'Golden Boys of the Ghetto.' *The New York Times Magazine,* 13 December 1981, pp. 55–8 *et seq.*

Phillips, B.J. 'Sugar Knows How to Hit, Man.' *Time,* 28 September 1981, pp. 68–9.

Putnam, Pat. 'Clearing the Way for the Big Payday.' *Sports Illustrated,* 15 July 1981, pp. 20–3.

The Day the Gold Turned Green.' *Sports Illustrated,* 14 February 1977, pp. 18–19.

'Fighting Is What I Do Best.' *Sports Illustrated,* 19 December 1983, p. 9.

'Finch Was a Pigeon for Sugar Ray.' *Sports Illustrated,* 1 March 1982, pp. 18–19.

'For Leonard It Was Down, and Then Out.' *Sports Illustrated,* 21 May 1984, pp. 38–9.

'Sugar Ray.' *Sports Illustrated,* 26 November 1979, pp. 92–6 *et seq.*

'An Uncertain View of the Future.' *Sports Illustrated,* 24 May 1982, pp. 48–52 *et seq.*

Quinn, Hal. 'A Legend in Crumbling Stone.' *Macleans,* 8 December 1980, pp. 32–3.

'The Lord of the Ring.' *Macleans,* 30 June 1980, p. 34.

Reilly, Rick. 'One Will Be Made Whole.' *Sports Illustrated,* 30 March 1987, pp. 58–64 *et seq.*

Schruers, Fred. 'Sugar Ray Leonard, Inc.' *Rolling Stone,* 26 June 1980, pp. 41–4.

'Sugar Ray Leonard, An Eddie Robinson Fan, Gifts $250G's To Grambling.' *Jet,* 13 July 1987, p. 50.

'Sugar Ray Retires to Promote Garden Bouts,' *Jet,* 7 September 1987, p. 46.

'Sugar's Sweet Comeback.' *People,* 20 April 1987, p. 41.

'A Super Finish to a Super Fight.' *Macleans,* 20 April 1987, p. 46.

'Sweet Smell of Success May Keep Sugar Swinging.' *Jet*, 27 April 1987, p. 48.

Unger, Norman O. 'A House Divided: The Sugar Ray Leonard Family.' *Ebony*, March 1984, pp. 27–8 *et seq.*

'Baby Jarrel Takes Over Ex-Champ's Happy Home.' *Ebony*, July 1985, p. 90 *et seq.*

'Savoring the Sweet Smell of Success.' *Ebony*, March 1980, pp. 66–8 *et seq.*

'Sugar Ray Faces Biggest Fight – Outside the Ring.' *Ebony*, July 1982, pp. 27–9 *et seq.*

'Who is the Greatest? A Tough Little Man Wins the Championship and the Title.' *People*, 25 January 1981, p. 42.

Wooten, James. 'The Lost Weekend of Sugar Ray Leonard.' *Esquire*, November 1984, p. 106 *et seq.*

Ziegel, Vic. 'A Second Chance for Sugar Ray.' *New York*, 1 December 1980, pp. 20–1.

Newspapers

Chicago Tribune
Gainesville (Florida) Sun
New York Daily News
New York Post
The New York Times

Ephemera

Berger, Phil, 'Ray Leonard,' *The New York Times Biographical Service*, June 1979, pp. 816–20.

'Leonard, Sugar Ray,' *Current Biography*, February 1981, pp. 25–8.

Smith, Red, 'Boxer and the Lady,' *The New York Times Biographical Service*, December 1979, p. 1683.

Index

E

F

G

H

I

J